EMERSON'S DEMANDING OPTIMISM

Emerson's Demanding Optimism

Gertrude Reif Hughes

LOUISIANA STATE UNIVERSITY PRESS

BATON ROUGE AND LONDON

FOR PAUL AND MARIA REIF

Copyright © 1984 by Gertrude Reif Hughes
All rights reserved
Manufactured in the United States of America
Designer: Barbara Werden
Typeface: Linotron Sabon
Typesetter: G & S Typesetters, Inc.

Excerpts from "Notes Toward a Supreme Fiction," by Wallace Stevens, in *Collected Poems of Wallace Stevens* are reprinted by permission of Alfred A. Knopf, Inc., to whom grateful acknowledgment is here offered. The author gratefully acknowledges permission of Little Brown and Company to quote from *The Complete Poems of Emily Dickinson*, edited by Thomas H. Johnson, Poems #370 and 569 Copyright 1929 by Martha Dickinson Bianchi; Copyright renewed 1957 by Mary L. Hampson; and Poem #346 Copyright 1935 by Martha Dickinson Bianchi; Copyright © renewed 1963 by Mary L. Hampson. Acknowledgment is also made to the publishers and the Trustees of Amherst College, for the use of Poems #569 and 346 from *The Poems of Emily Dickinson*, edited by Thomas H. Johnson, Cambridge, Mass.: The Belknap Press of Harvard University Press, Copyright © 1951, © 1955, 1979, 1983 by the President and Fellows of Harvard College; reprinted by permission.

LIBRARY OF CONGRESS CATALOGING IN PUBLICATION DATA

Hughes, Gertrude Reif.
  Emerson's demanding optimism.

  Bibliography: p.
  Includes index.
    1. Emerson, Ralph Waldo, 1803–1882—Criticism and interpretation.
2. Optimism in literature. 3. Verification (Logic) in literature. 4. Belief and doubt in literature. I. Title.
PS1642.O5H84 1984   814'.3   84-7167
ISBN 0-8071-1180-5

Contents

Abbreviations   vii

Preface   ix

Acknowledgments   xv

CHAPTER I   Cost as Confirmation: *The Conduct of Life*   1

CHAPTER II   Poverty as Adequate Desire: "Experience"   35

CHAPTER III   Leasts and Lustres: Emerson's Fables   66

CHAPTER IV   The Risks of Affirmation: "Compensation" and "Self-Reliance"   95

CHAPTER V   "Original Relation": *Nature* and Correspondence   132

Bibliography   171

Index   179

Abbreviations

FOR convenience, the following abbreviations are used in the text to identify sources of material quoted from Emerson's writings:

CW   *The Collected Works of Ralph Waldo Emerson*, Vol. I: *Nature, Addresses, and Lectures*, ed. Robert E. Spiller and Alfred R. Ferguson. Cambridge: Harvard University Press, 1971.

EL   *The Early Lectures of Ralph Waldo Emerson*, ed. Stephen E. Whicher, Robert E. Spiller, and Wallace E. Williams. 3 vols. Cambridge: Harvard University Press, 1959, 1964, 1972.

J   *The Journals of Ralph Waldo Emerson*, ed. Edward Waldo Emerson and Waldo Emerson Forbes. 10 vols. Boston and New York: Houghton Mifflin, 1909–14.

JMN   *The Journals and Miscellaneous Notebooks of Ralph Waldo Emerson*, ed. William H. Gilman, Alfred R. Ferguson, George P. Clark, Merrell R. Davis, Merton M. Sealts, Harrison Hayford, Ralph H. Orth, J. E. Parsons, A. W. Plumstead, Linda Allardt, and Susan Sutton Smith. 14 vols. Cambridge: Harvard University Press, 1960–.

W   *The Complete Works of Ralph Waldo Emerson*, Centenary Edition. 12 vols. Boston and New York: Houghton Mifflin and Co., 1903–1904.

Preface

EMERSON'S reputation as America's foremost purveyor of affirmation is both accurate and misleading. He is known correctly as the visionary Yankee for whom the order of the universe was so thoroughly democratic that "one design unites and animates the farthest pinnacle and the lowest trench" (W, I, 112; CW, I, 68). For him even the humblest person or fact embodied divinity. As a consequence, all individuals could trust themselves to explore and develop the still "unsearched might of men" that was present in each of them (W, I, 114; CW, I, 69). Unfortunately his famous confidence in the perfectability of every individual disposes readers to enshrine Emerson as a sage or condescend to him as a relic of simpler, more harmonious times. Even readers who acknowledge his greatness and grant his undeniable influence on American life and letters mistrust his hopefulness.

No one was more aware than Emerson himself of the nervous pulse-taking prompted by his faith in individual promise, in what he called "the infinitude of the private man." "The fate of my books," he wrote in his 1850 journal, "is like the impression of my face. My acquaintances as long back as I can remember, have always said, 'seems to me you look a little thinner than when I saw you last'" (JMN, XI, 214–15). Emerson's rueful remark shrewdly identifies his public's inclination to assume that as he matured, his optimistic confidence must diminish, and the tendency to discover decline in America's prophet of possibility has continued to recur in the century since his death in 1882. A commonplace of Emerson scholarship holds that the early voice of rhapsodic affirmation and challenge gave way, after the death of little Waldo in 1842 or the Mexican war of 1846, to a voice that is more skeptical, or resigned, or just plain tired. This more resigned Emerson has had defenders and even champions. But the relationship between the heady Emerson whose first book challenged his readers, "Build, therefore, your own world" (W, I, 76; CW, I, 45), and the Emerson who acknowledged a quarter-century later that "Every spirit makes its house; but afterwards the house confines the spirit" (W, VI, 9) has persistently been seen in terms of decline.[1]

As I read Emerson's essays, however, the house's power to confine the spirit that built it demonstrates how strongly spirit builds, not how easily spirit may be constrained. The confinement is costly; there is no doubt about that. But Emerson offers this high cost as a confirmation. It confirms the articulating power, not the fragility of the world-building, house-making spirit that is Emerson's continuing subject. His affirmations of a common yet individual power are not locker-room pep talks or revival-meeting evangelism. His hoping is austere, his believing dire. The more one recognizes that his affirmations function as challenges rather than reassurances, the less one will chide his later work for seeming, like his face, "a little thinner" than expected. The more one learns to see the later works as confirmation not retraction of earlier beliefs, the more one will understand how demanding these beliefs were in the first place. For the promises Emerson offers do not reassure, they make demands. As he warned throughout his career, it can be costly to believe in individuals' essential divinity. The cost confirms the value, not the foolishness, of such a belief. Thus the supposed capitulations of later works like "Experience" and *The Conduct of Life* do not recant the bold faith of earlier works like "Self-Reliance," "Compensation," and *Nature*; rather the later essays articulate those earlier affirmations more fully.

1. For instances, see Stephen E. Whicher, *Freedom and Fate: An Inner Life of Ralph Waldo Emerson* (New York, 1953; rpt. Perpetua Edition, 1961), 164 and *passim*; Carl F. Strauch, "The Importance of Emerson's Skeptical Mood," *Harvard Library Bulletin*, 11 (Winter, 1957), 117–39; Strauch, "Emerson's Sacred Science," PMLA, 73 (June, 1958), 250; R. A. Yoder, "Toward the 'Titmouse Dimension': The Development of Emerson's Poetic Style," PMLA, 87 (March, 1972), 255–70; Yoder, "Emerson's Dialectic," *Criticism*, 11 (Fall, 1969), 314–28; Jonathan Bishop, *Emerson on the Soul* (Cambridge, Mass., 1964), 200, 216; Joel Porte, *Representative Man: Ralph Waldo Emerson in His Time* (New York, 1979), 279.

Locating and studying such costly confirmations as the one about spirit building so strongly that it confines itself reveals some peculiar characteristics of Emerson's quest for right relationship between ME and NOT ME. First, it is a search without being a journey. Certain from the start of "the infinitude of the private man," Emerson moves neither toward nor away from this initial conception. He moves within it. Second, though experience vitally affects him, it neither brings revelation nor dispels illusion. Rather, experience functions for Emerson as it does in Saint Paul's letter to the Romans; it is the cause of a hope that need not make for shame, because it is the result of an openness (Saint Paul calls it "patience") that is tempered rather than weakened by tribulation. "We glory in tribulations also: knowing that tribulation worketh patience; and patience, experience; and experience, hope: and hope maketh not ashamed" (Romans 5 : 3 – 5).

To reconceive the way experience functions for Emerson is to see that, instead of invalidating his affirmations, experience reveals their basic austerity. What has been affirmed out of conviction becomes confirmed by experience, even painful experience. The idea that the cost of faith can signal its validity rather than its fallaciousness is fundamental to such a transformation. In short, Emerson's maturity shows a growing awareness more than a changing conviction. Accordingly, there can be heard in all his work—early or late, formal essay or lecture, and informal notebook or journal—two voices, an affirming and a confirming one.

The relationship between affirmation and confirmation is subtle and volatile. Temporally of course, affirmation comes first. Without affirmation there can exist no confirmation, for where nothing has been projected nothing can be verified. Functionally, affirmation and confirmation work as complements each to the other. Without confirmation, what has been affirmed, believed, hoped, announced, or promised remains incompletely known. Confirmation not only validates existing belief or thought, it also constitutes a revelation of what the original thought or belief entailed. Because confirmation can only reveal retrospectively, this book begins with *The Conduct of Life* (1860), instead of with *Nature* (1836). This unorthodox procedure permits me to work toward the characteristic affirmations of *Nature*, "Self-Reliance," and "Compensation" rather than away from them. By putting Emerson's headiest affirmations in the context of their soberest confirmations, I mean to show how durable, flexible, and realistic his "optimism" is.

Aside from being efficacious, it seems peculiarly apt to suspend chronology in Emerson's case. His breakdown did not come until 1872, ten years before his death and twelve years of continuing if steadily diminishing professional activity after the publication of *The Conduct of Life*. Just as that book, published in 1860, was the work of a not-yet-declining genius, so his first book, *Nature*, published in 1836, was the work of an already mature one. After all, when Emerson first published *Nature* at the age of thirty-three, he had already embraced and abandoned his first vocation, married and lost his first wife, lost also his brother Edward and his most beloved brother Charles, as well as having lost his father during boyhood. In addition, Emerson was sufficiently well known in 1836 to be recognized as the author of *Nature* even though his name did not appear on the title page of the first edition. It makes sense, then, to regard all Emerson's major writings as products of the prime of his long life, and to feel that the chronology within that scant quarter-century may be safely set aside in the interest of assessing how Emerson's powers of consolidation enhance and complete his powers of affirmation.[2]

Suffering has made hope seem naïve and frivolous to many people, but there is also an emerging sense that inner and outer wastelands are not the only landscapes around and that visionaries are not necessarily escapists. Cynicism, angst, and existential dread may now be perpetuating the outrages they originally registered. It seems that pacifists, feminists, young people, and individuals at large are beginning to suspect this and to want to rescue hope from the bad reputation that social upheavals and atrocities have given it. Yet a society ready to abandon despair can be seduced by facile optimism. That is why Emerson's style

2. For an excellent discussion of Emerson's consolidating power see Maurice Gonnaud, *Individu et Société dans L'Oeuvre de Ralph Waldo Emerson: Essai de Biographie Spirituelle* (Paris, 1964), 415–16, 443–46.

of hoping and believing should be recognized; it can both challenge and empower an incipient desire for alternatives to despair. In his study of literary transcendentalism Lawrence I. Buell observed that "the student of nonfictional literature must be prepared to show why the thought of an Emerson or an Arnold leads irresistibly to strongly poetic or rhetorical forms of expression." [3] Emerson's prose invites rhetorical study. [4] He designed it to challenge and hearten. It does not stoop to persuade, and it offers neither exemplary narratives of how to live nor systematic constructions of truth. Although every essay announces some form of his lifelong belief in individuals' access to the universally available power he sometimes calls the "Over-Soul," he constructs each one to invigorate rather than convince his audience, because "the one thing in the world of value, is, the active soul," not assent or dissent (W, I, 90; CW, I, 56). Accordingly, I have no desire to defend doctrines Emerson may be supposed to hold. My own hope for this study of Emerson's styles of hoping is that it will help readers to use his prose for the reinvigoration he wanted to foster.

---

3. Lawrence I. Buell, *Literary Transcendentalism: Style and Vision in the American Renaissance* (Ithaca, N.Y., 1973), 13.
4. For a discussion of rhetorical criticism see Wayne Booth, *The Rhetoric of Fiction* (Chicago, 1961), 71–76, 119–44, 211–21, 395–96, and *passim*.

Acknowledgments

I WISH TO THANK Wesleyan University for supporting this book with a sabbatical and with grant funds. Thanks are also due Alice Pomper for typing and retyping the manuscript, and Beverly Jarrett and John Easterly of Louisiana State University Press for giving it scrupulous and friendly editing.

I am grateful to teachers, friends, and colleagues who read and offered comments on all or part of the work at various stages: Barbara Currier Bell, Harold Bloom, Philip P. Hallie, Geraldine Murphy, Richard Ohmann, Joseph W. Reed, Jr., Phyllis Rose, Richard Slotkin, Gail Tubbs, Alfred Turco, Jr., and Elisabeth Young-Bruehl.

The book is dedicated to my late parents in gratitude for their contributions to its growth and mine. For encouragement, I am grateful to my former husband, Robert G. Hughes. Finally, for cooperation and the happiness they give, I thank our children: Timothy, Kenneth, Paul, and Lucy.

EMERSON'S DEMANDING OPTIMISM

I

Cost as Confirmation:
The Conduct of Life

*The wonderful synthesis so familiar in nature; the up-
per and the under side of the medal of Jove; the union
of impossibilities, which reappears in every object; its
real and its ideal power,—was now also transferred entire to the consciousness of a man.*
*. . . Plato turns incessantly the obvers and the reverse
of the medal of Jove.* ("Plato; or, The Philosopher," W,
IV, 54–56)

*Every fact is related on one side to sensation and on the
other to morals. The game of thought is, on the appearance of one of these two sides, to find the other; given
the upper, to find the under side. Nothing so thin but
has these two faces, and when the observer has seen the
obverse, he turns it over to see the reverse. Life is a
pitching of this penny,—heads or tails. We never tire of
this game, because there is still a slight shudder of astonishment at the exhibition of the other face, at the
contrast of the two faces.* ("Montaigne; or, The Skeptic," W, IV, 149)

 MERSON's terms for describing
mental activity are the same
whether he is picturing Plato's
genius for synthesis or Montaigne's for doubt. The two-
faced coin serves to illustrate both kinds of thinking, as the passages above show. Efficiently, it includes the various qualities
that thinking has for Emerson: its office of reconciliation, its
character of surprise, its destiny always to be as old as the impossible and as new as the potential. The medal of Jove is the coin of
the Emersonian realm. Not even a superficial reader of Emerson
is unaware that his arguments progress by contraries, that his
two eyes—the one Yankee, the other visionary—make one in
sight, and that polarity and paradox are as much his medium as

his message. Common as this recognition may be, *The Conduct of Life* is rich in unjustly neglected transactions involving the medal of Jove. It reveals on nearly every page the relationship between the Emerson of *Nature*, who challenges, "Build therefore your own World," and the Emerson who knows that to build your own world is to proceed to have to live in it.

The Conduct of Life is "Emerson's most sophisticated book in terms of literary structure," and the last one to be entirely composed by Emerson himself without the editorial assistance of James Elliot Cabot.[1] In *The Conduct of Life* Emerson pays tribute, in the sense both of payment and of celebration, to his own earliest certainties. That payment is made by a process of not only continually flipping the medal of Jove, but repeatedly reminting it. Charles Feidelson points out that "Emerson worked the sum over and over, starting from scratch every time."[2] Feidelson refers to Emerson's method of dealing with the recurring, recalcitrant problem posed by the difficulty of maintaining focus when every unity is bipolar as surely as every bipolarity is a unity. But Feidelson's figure is also apt as a description of the quiet bravery with which Emerson characteristically meets not only the requirements imposed by his method of seeing but those imposed also by its result. That quiet bravery should not be interpreted as desperation or abdication but as patience and tenacity.

The neglected central chapter of *The Conduct of Life*, "Behavior," opens with, "The soul which animates nature is not less significantly published in the figure, the movement and the gesture of animated bodies, than in its last vehicle [, that] of articulated speech."

At the very outset, behavior or manners is presented as a language, the language of the body. It follows that best behavior, or grace in manners, is eloquence. Emerson opens by placing his topic with care, daring, and originality, but he does this so quietly that it is easy to miss the implications. He is choosing to discuss behavior in terms of eloquence, an art that he equated

1. Buell, *Literary Transcendentalism*, 162.
2. Charles Feidelson, Jr., *Symbolism and American Literature* (Chicago, 1953), 126.

with divinity itself.[3] "Eloquence . . . is the best speech of the best soul. It may well stand as the exponent of all that is grand and immortal in the mind" (W, VII, 99). Once he has related behavior to speech, he proceeds to indicate that "this silent and subtle language is manners; not *what*, but *how*" (Emerson's italics). He means much more than content and form or matter and method by this *what* and *how*. And his essay "Eloquence," which was probably delivered as a lecture in 1847 in about the form in which it survives as chapter three of *Society and Solitude*, provides the gloss necessary to appreciate what is at stake.[4] In a long, stern, rhapsodic final passage in that essay Emerson announces that a difficult blend of *what* and *how* constitutes true eloquence (W, VII, 91–93). First, the requirement for a *what* sufficient to make its own *how*, that is, the requirement for a meter-making argument:

> In cases where profound conviction has been wrought, the eloquent man is he who is no beautiful speaker, but who is inwardly drunk with a certain belief. It agitates and tears him. . . . Then it rushes from him as in short, abrupt screams, in torrents of meaning. The possession the subject has of his mind is so entire that it insures an order of expression which is the order of Nature itself, and so the order of the greatest force, and inimitable by any art. . . . [The speaker's] mind is contemplating a whole, and inflamed by the contemplation of the whole, and . . . the words and sentences uttered by him, however admirable, fall from him as unregarded parts of that terrible whole which he sees and which he means that you shall see.

Rem tene verba sequentur, but notice the risk and the terror required to hold, or rather to be held by, one's topic. Nor is such submission to the hold of one's topic sufficient to generate a truly

---

3. Compare Harold Bloom's cognate point in "The Freshness of Transformation, or Emerson on Influence," in David Levin (ed.), *Emerson: Prophecy, Metamorphosis, and Influence* (New York, 1975), 129–48, especially p. 135. See also Porte, *Representative Man*, 293–96.
4. See Edward Emerson's introductory note, W, VII, 364.

eloquent *how*: "Add to this concentration a certain regnant calmness, which, in all the tumult, never utters a premature syllable, but keeps the secret of its means and method; and the orator stands before the people as a demoniacal power to whose miracles they have no key." Emerson does not trouble himself to disclose from what source that regnant calmness is to be drawn (though in the 1867 essay on eloquence, in *Letters and Social Aims*, it is clear, as in the earlier essay, that the source is one's readiness, one's presence of mind, a life—presumably—of preparedness, if not of preparation, that has to do with veneration for facts and daily events over speculation and learnedness). Emerson is not interested in the source for this added *how*, but in its necessity and its power to make the speaker demoniacal and a miracle. The next and last sentence of his rhapsody on the tragic intensity of eloquence places into a pagan and dramatic setting the entire meditation on eloquence as a power. "This terrible earnestness makes good the ancient superstition of the hunter, that the bullet will hit its mark, which is first dipped in the marksman's blood." If the *what* is the bullet, the *how* is, at least partly, the marksman's own blood. Such a passage gives a deep seriousness to the assertion in "Behavior" that manners are a language, a *how* rather than a *what*. To ignore that seriousness would be to ignore the centrality of the chapter and ultimately the weight of the whole book.

The *what* and the *how* of behavior are, then, to be the two faces of the medal of Jove which Emerson is about to pitch and remint. Although he claims at the outset to have settled the question of content and form, matter and manner in favor of the *how*, it is of course not long before Emerson uses the separation to demonstrate a unity. For he now introduces the fablelike description of John Quincy Adams as the senator with the orderly and forceful will beneath the weak and irritable exterior, acknowledging that a *how* may conceal rather than reveal. The vignette of Gertrude and Blanche, in which Blanche's character is more eloquent than Gertrude's grace, further weakens his initial argument that the body's language never lies. Of course it lies, and Emerson purposely loses several such tosses of the coin in order to establish that the only *how* worthy of consideration is the *how* that precisely suits a *what*. Having taken pains to show that *how* is distinct from *what*, he uses the distinction to disclaim interest in its chief import. For Emerson is interested in the abiding readability not the possible autonomy of behavior. The surprises connected with that readability constitute the middle of the essay, but the end of the essay effects a new formulation as characteristically unpredictable as it is ineluctably characteristic: Behavior as style is not an exterior index of an interior state; it is a use by an individual of his own individuality; it is . . . self-reliance. "For it is not what talents or genius a man has, but how he is to his talents, that constitutes friendship and character" (W, VI, 193). With this announcement, obverse and reverse have been made to disappear. Inside and outside, hidden and revealed, have been melted into fluidity. The very next sentence mints the new coin: "The man that stands by himself, the universe stands by him also."[5] Equating an ablative of means with an ablative of accompaniment yields the rule for behavior: Your means as an individual *are* your place in the world, in the world of human beings, in nature, even in the cosmos. The entire NOT-ME *is* ME (or is *for* ME) when, and only when, I am a means that is a power.

Of course it is hardly surprising that self-reliance (or correspondence, or compensation) should be the hard-won conclusion of an Emerson essay. Nor is there need for yet another critic who wins through to reecho the insight that Emerson uses duality to make unity. Although the above explication of "Behavior" unavoidably details these Emersonian processes, its purpose has been more than a description of the text. Its purpose has been to introduce and substantiate two features of the text: first, that the essay is neither resigned nor homely but rather central in both the arithmetical and the Emersonian senses; second, that the relationship between the essay's beginning and its end is characteristic of the other chapters in *The Conduct of Life*. The first claim is self-evident from the explication, with its use of "Eloquence" as gloss. But the second requires further attention.

5. Compare the exchange between Feste and Viola concerning language and corruption which begins with the question whether Feste lives by his labor or lives by the church. *Twelfth Night*, III, i, 1–26.

THE RELATIONSHIP between beginnings and endings in Emerson's essays, as in his entire career, can be obscured by his reputation. Although celebrated for his putative doctrines of ascendancy, relied upon for his capacity to uplift his hearers as an orator, and renowned as the champion of a compensation that meant You will be rewarded, not You shall be charged, Emerson should not be read as though he wrote like the "scholar of the first age" described in the "American Scholar" address of 1837: "The scholar of the first age received into him the world around; brooded thereon, gave it the new arrangement of his own mind, —and uttered it again. It came into him life; it went out from him truth" (W, I, 87).

Certainly Emerson's essays end with an intensity that could be called truth, and they begin with a relative deliberateness that could be called life. But the "new arrangement of his own mind" has been tried out in the journals and notebooks, and then tested before lecture audiences until this new arrangement is itself a truth, for Emerson, that permits him to write far more deductively than the formula from "The American Scholar" suggests. The essays do not follow this formula. That formula would tend to yield an essay whose beginning is more tentative than its end, and whose end is more definitive, perhaps more static, certainly more liable to discursive assessment, than its beginning. Such an essay on behavior might be expected to begin with examples of all kinds of behavior—from the meanest to the most heroic, or from the most deceptive to the most honorable—and then to evaluate these by way of articulating a concluding abstraction about behavior, perhaps that a man's behavior is the clue to his inner state. Whether or not behavior was held to be a reliable index of character, whether or not it was held to be an honorable feature of the whole man, whether behavior-as-meaning was held to be a pity, a wonder, or an impossibility, such an essay would have started, progressed, and ended very differently from the one Emerson actually wrote.

The distinctive features of Emerson's essay on behavior are these: It begins by defining behavior according to its relations, its kinship as a language with eloquence; it proceeds, as would the hypothetical essay, by examples, but these are examples of the workings of a dynamic relationship rather than the inventories of "things added to things" that Emerson condemns as infertile and therefore unpoetic in his essay on Plato (W, IV, 56). The conclusion of "Behavior" is a power more than it is a truth, just as its beginning has been concerned with truth more than with life. It may, then, not be too perverse to say that the Emersonian essay comes into him truth and goes out from him life, instead of recording and enacting the process Emerson describes in the sentences from the Phi Beta Kappa address. The Emersonian essay is an exercise in the sublime as Emerson defines it in "Worship": "To make our word or act sublime we must make it real" (W, VI, 226). The important thing is not to quibble over distinctions between truth and life, but to see that the Emersonian essay ends with power and to recognize as fully as possible the ramifications of that fact.

Whether such concluding power is more suitably called truth or life or neither, it is an end designed to create its readers more than to instruct or even persuade them.[6] "What is best in literature is the affirming, prophesying, spermatic words of men-making poets. Only that is poetry which cleanses and mans me" (W, VIII, 294). A meter-making argument must be men-making if it is to be worthy of the name of poetry. This standard and this mission are the ones to which Emerson dedicates himself in his familiar disclaimer,

> I have been writing and speaking what were once called novelties, for twenty-five or thirty years, and have not now one disciple. Why? Not that what I said was not true; not that it has not won intelligent receivers; but because it did not go from any wish in me to bring men to me, but to themselves. I delight in driving them from me. What could I do, if they came to me?—they would interrupt and encumber me. This is my

6. For a related argument see Roland F. Lee, "Emerson Through Kierkegaard: Toward a Definition of Emerson's Theory of Communication," ELH, 24 (1957), 229–48. See also David M. Wyatt, "Spelling Time: The Reader in Emerson's 'Circles,'" *American Literature*, 48, 2 (1976), 140–51, for a specific application of a cognate idea.

boast that I have no school follower. I should account it a measure of the impurity of insight, if it did not create independence. (J, IX, 186)[7]

The essays in *The Conduct of Life* offer perhaps the clearest record and the most moving enactment of what it is to attempt this sort of men-making poetry. "Fate," "Power," "Wealth," "Culture," "Behavior," "Worship," "Considerations by the Way," "Beauty," "Illusion"—each of the book's nine chapters transforms its topic with the aim of invigorating its readers. Just as behavior is not manners but manner, that is style, or language-used, so fate is not circumstance but self; power is not dominion but obedience; wealth is not possession but husbandry; worship is neither faith nor skepticism but cosmically aligned thinking; beauty and culture are symptoms of ameliorating laws, not results either of creation or striving; illusions are not deceptions but protections. Even the purportedly miscellaneous considerations by the way turn out to be nothing less than considerations *of* The Way, of its creative catastrophes, its fresh availability for each new traveller, its "populous solitude" that suggests and therefore requires that to travel this Way is to stand still and prepare to be found (W, VI, 269, 278). Such transformations are the stuff of Emerson's book, but stuff is the wrong word. They are its means in both senses: its method and its riches. "To be rich is to have a ticket of admission to the masterworks and chief men of each race" (W, VI, 94), as Emerson puts it in "Wealth."

The Emersonian man of means is, of course, the man of power, the person with a reliable and relying self. But the terms of the old Emersonian sum are once again curious when he comes to write the essay entitled "Wealth." Its beginning, like that of "Behavior," demonstrates Emerson's characteristic use of openings. There is a surprising and important freshness at the start. Instead of starting on a low plane with examples of mate-

7. Compare "We hear eagerly every thought and word quoted from an intellectual man. But in his presence our own mind is roused to activity, and we forget very fast what he says, much more interested in the new play of our own thought than in any thought of his" W, VI, 26.

rial wealth and then going on to show that material wealth is false and only spiritual treasure can be laid up, the whole idea of laying up treasure of any kind is called into question at the outset: "Every man is a consumer and ought to be a producer. He fails to make his place good in the world unless he not only pays his debt but also adds something to the common wealth. Nor can he do justice to his genius without making some larger demand on the world than base subsistence. He is by constitution expensive and needs to be rich."

Instantly we are in the realm of paradox and pun. To make his place good is, of course, to make good his place (as the reference to debt-paying verifies), but it is also to improve his place. To pay that second kind of debt he must earn, and paradoxically, such earning is "making some large demand." To make good is to be good; to be good is to do justice not to some ethical command but to the demand of one's genius. That demand is an expensive one, and therefore one must be rich. One must be rich in order to be worthy of one's precious individuality. How much is a rich man worth? As much as he is able to expend in order to earn his livelihood, pay for his life, and certify that his life is his alone.

Later in the essay Emerson offers a definition of value that combines his Yankee shrewdness with his visionary insouciance. What is value? Not marketability as the cynic might say; not some intrinsic worth as the optimist might wish; but risk: "If a St. Michael's pear sells for a shilling, it costs a shilling to raise it. . . . The shilling represents the number of enemies the pear has, and the amount of risk in ripening it" (W, VI, 108). Cost, then, is neither something as arbitrary as the going rate nor as static as a price-to-be-exacted. It is risk, a dynamic but predictable relationship between expenditure and income. Exact, if exacting of the self, dependable, if dependent upon the self, risk is itself a paradox and so, therefore, are cost and value. For where there is expensiveness there is need—the need to be rich; and only where such need is truly felt is there that poverty, that neediness of spirit, which is the vacuum that the necessary, provident means can rush to fill.

It is inevitable and telling that a discussion of Emersonian wealth should lead so quickly to considerations of Emersonian poverty, but let those considerations be postponed for now. As I have been showing, Emerson opposes production to consumption in order to provide himself with the polarity necessary for argument. In doing so, he chooses the pole of productivity. He announces that its relationship to wealth is the neglected one and makes the announcement in a paragraph so bristling with paradox and pun that its declaration that every man ought to be a producer not a consumer turns into a veritable charge. Never one to leave his audience without means, though famously willing to leave us without explanation, Emerson proceeds from charge to enabling analysis: "Wealth has its source in applications of the mind to nature, from the rudest strokes of spade and axe up to the last secrets of art. Intimate ties subsist between thought and all production" (W, VI, 85).

The sequence sets up the true tensions that will produce the essay and engender its characteristic result. Subsistence of those intimate ties between thought and all production makes it necessary for Emerson to counsel production over consumption and makes it possible for him to mean by wealth not only a making rather than a hoarding but thinking and transforming rather than establishing and possessing. "Men of sense esteem wealth to be the assimilation of nature to themselves, the converting of the sap and juices of the planet to the incarnation and nutriment of the design" (W, VI, 93).

Identifying the ties between thinking and producing permits Emerson to proffer numerous practical corollaries concerning pricing, farming, and economic history that are both shrewdly accurate in their purported application and accurately symbolic in their intended evocation. These more worldly considerations are versions of the initial dictum that wealth is of the mind. Their practicality depends upon Emerson's having placed them under the paradoxical, spiritual heading we have been examining, and they have the force not of advice but of exemplification.

As the essay's second half proceeds through its five numbered "measures of economy," the near-redundancy of their concepts combines with their rhetorical variety to create that Emersonian fusion of unity and diversity that consolidates even as it extends and clarifies even as it complicates. "Each man's expense [*i.e.*, expenditure] must proceed from his character" goes the first maxim, recapitulated and extended by the second: "Spend after your genius, *and by system*" (Emerson's italics). These versions of economic self-reliance owe their import, their evocative power, less to any irrefutable sagacity than to the ties between thinking and production that Emerson has already established. So also with the next two maxims—"*Impera parendo*" (command by obeying), and "look for seed of the same kind as you sow"—during which pronouncements self-reliance becomes correspondence imperceptibly, inevitably, and reassuringly. Nor is the sequence complete until correspondence has become compensation in the fifth maxim, "Spend for power and not for pleasure," its Puritan negative transvalued by the transcendental affirmative. The point is not that Emersonian themes should be present in an essay by Emerson, but that Emersonian techniques both promote and actually are these themes.

From the moment he initiates his argument in terms of production versus consumption, going on to ally production with thinking and transforming rather than with establishing and instituting, Emerson has insured a characteristic and difficult coherence for his argument. This coherence is not the fluency so many have deplored the absence of and some few have loyally tried to demonstrate.[8] Nor is this coherence that of the house patiently built up from foundation to attic—a house from which the architect may sometimes unfortunately have omitted the stairs, to paraphrase Emerson's own complaint about the lack of coherence in his essays.[9] Rather, this coherence is that of a gathering, a community. Emerson argues by placement, by arrangement, more than by development. As little deployed for explanation as for consistency, more suited to suggestion than definition,

8. See especially Lawrence I. Buell, "Reading Emerson for the Structures: The Coherence of the Essays," *Quarterly Review of Speech*, 58 (February, 1972), 56–69.

9. "I found out when I had finished my lecture that it was a very good house, only the architect had unfortunately omitted the stairs" (J, VIII, 167).

Emerson's technique is not to draw a line, nor even to cultivate a growth. It is both more instantaneous and more imperious, less methodical and less predictable, than even the cultivation metaphor would suggest. His technique is to create a firmament and then populate it. To bring about the coherence of his essays, Emerson collects concepts and examples, letting their juxtaposition generate the drama of argument. But he does more than this. He first calls into being the place within which this gathering is to happen, and he does so by the pronouncement of laws, rather than by rhetorical labor.

"What a *fiat lux* is there!" was Carlyle's enthusiastic response to *The Conduct of Life*.[10] I take *fiat* to be the operative word here. Let there be light. Let X equal this. Let behavior be eloquence, wealth be transformation, beauty be perceived relatedness, power be obedience. With a beginning that is already a construct, a solid rather than a point, Emerson proceeds by using that three-dimensional space to house what it can, taking less thought about what will fit (since almost anything might) than about how it will fit, given the initial shape. The resulting coherence is that of the oxymoronic "populous solitude" of "Considerations by the Way," a plenitude of isolates made significant not only by the fact of their gathering but by the occasion that the essay's opening creates. To put it most briefly, Emerson's beginnings are climactic and his endings initiative.

With its defiant, even defensive, opening diatribe, and its prophetic conclusion, "Worship" seems to contradict this assertion. Actually, however, the essay's opening tests the rule and reveals it to be sound. If Emerson had written "Worship" according to the formula from the "American Scholar" address that seems so likely to describe Emerson's own technique, it might have begun with some examples of local piety, some references to daily acts of devotion common to any believing citizen, some enumera-

10. Joseph Slater (ed.), *The Correspondence of Emerson and Carlyle* (New York and London, 1964), 534, hereinafter cited as Slater (ed.), *Correspondence*. Actually, Carlyle's exclamation refers only to the famous fable that concludes "Illusions," but his response to the entire book was so enthusiastic that his exclamation of praise may be taken to refer to the whole work. Edward Emerson quotes the letter in W, VI, 336.

tions of conventional religious forms and their inadequacies and superfluities relative to the common citizen's personal faith. From here, he might be expected to move to a celebration of individual divinity over institutionalized divinity, ending with a ringing affirmation compounded of hope for self-reliance, love for correspondence, and faith in compensation. Having started where he found his audience, he would have brought them step by step to a higher plane while at the same time asserting that, potentially, they had been on that plane all along. However, though these subjects and convictions are to be found in the essay, its actual course is quite different from this description.

Like the other chapters, "Worship" begins by placing its topic among surprising relations. That placement is less surprising for the terms invoked than for the reversal that is insisted upon. His terms for the discussion of behavior belonged as much to eloquence as to conduct, being Emerson's way of placing that apparently pedestrian subject among exalted relations. Emerson made the subject of wealth dynamic instead of static by choosing a dialectic between production and consumption, with production becoming a matter of spiritual use rather than of material proliferation. But here Emerson takes an apparently sacred topic, worship, and places it among apparently profane relations. Whereas in "Wealth" and "Behavior" the placement gives weight to the deliberations, in "Worship" the placement gives vigor and body to what might otherwise remain immaterial— the ironic fate, Emerson knew, of approaching spirit by excluding matter. Precisely to avoid being immaterial, even at the risk of being charged with materialism, Emerson is at pains to announce that skepticism and faith, like materiality and spirituality, are not incompatible but mutually supporting.

Indeed, the beginning of "Worship" is a stern, even angry, defense against charges that the author of *The Conduct of Life* has conducted his inquiries from "too low a platform" (W, VI, 201). Already in the second chapter, "Power," he seems aware of his audience's impatience: "I have not forgotten that there are sublime considerations which limit the value of talent and superficial success," he says, apparently anticipating objections to his supposed emphasis on "low" instances of power. "There are sources on which we have not drawn," he goes on to assure his audience, ending all-but-haughtily with, "I know what I abstain from. I adjourn what I have to say on this topic to the chapter on Culture and Worship" (W, VI, 80). In the fourth chapter, on culture, he does offer the promised corrective by introducing in its opening paragraph the important proviso that "a man is the prisoner of his power. A topical memory makes him an almanac; a talent for debate, a disputant; skill to get money makes him a miser, that is, a beggar. Culture reduces these inflammations by invoking the aid of other powers against the dominant talent, and by appealing to the rank of powers" (W, VI, 131). But it is not until chapter six, when his subject is worship, that it serves Emerson best to dwell at some length and with great vigor on his audience's mistaken expectations.

For this essay he reserves his famous defiance, "I dip my pen into the blackest ink, because I am not afraid of falling into my inkpot" (W, VI, 201). In this essay he seeks to silence the cavils of a querulous audience, exposing the faithlessness of their alleged complaints by sternly articulating the dangers of fearing skepticism. The accusation of a skepticism enforced by candor is really an accusation that faith cannot comport with honesty, Emerson shows. Either too proud or too wise—or, probably, both—to refer his audience to the celebration of courage with which he inaugurated the chapter on power, Emerson here concentrates on revealing that fear of skepticism is infidelity to faith, and that it enervates rather than purifies beliefs. As George Macdonald is later to write in the long poem "The Disciple," "The man that feareth Lord to doubt / In that fear doubteth thee."[11] It serves Emerson's purposes perfectly to use the opening of "Worship" to expose the faithlessness behind his audience's dissatisfaction, because opening this way enables him to reverse his topic. Not worship but the worshipper must be his concern in this essay, because, as he says on the fifth page of his thirteen-page polemic, "religion cannot rise above the state of the votary" (W, VI, 205).

11. George Macdonald, *A Hidden Life and Other Poems* (New York, 1872), 91.

The state of the votary is to be Emerson's true subject then, and the two sides of this state are the votary's capacity to do and say on the one hand, versus his capacity to suffer and hear on the other. Or they are speaking and knowing, or they are working and being.

The association of behavior with language is familiar from "Behavior," as is the association between speech and divinity; and these associations are certainly central to the book as a whole. But "Worship" bears closest resemblances to "Fate" and to "Montaigne." These important resemblances reveal Emerson's distinctive, oxymoronic attitude of rebellious resignation, or insouciant reliance, or scrupulous abandon. Far from being an attitude that denies belief or retreats from affirmation, it is an attitude that takes fullest account of what has been affirmed, testing its soundness rather than limiting its application. It is the attitude toward the cost, risk, and value of believing that I refer to as "Confirmation."

The resemblance to "Montaigne" is striking because it includes self-quotation. When the opening diatribe finally exhausts itself, Emerson returns to principle-stating, the mode with which he usually begins an essay and the mode which he could not sustain at the beginning of this one, because angry exemplification had to accomplish what his serene opening could not be trusted to do. That assertion of principle, "I am sure that a certain truth will be said through me, though I should be dumb, or though I should try to say the reverse" (W, VI, 201), continues after the polemical interruption I have been discussing. "There is a principle which is the basis of things, which all speech aims to say, and all action to evolve, a simple, quiet, undescribed, undescribable presence dwelling very peacefully in us, our rightful lord: we are not to do, but to let do; not to work, but to be worked upon" (W, VI, 213). That last phrase is borrowed verbatim from the final paragraph of "Montaigne."

Let a man learn to look for the permanent in the mutable and fleeting; let him learn to bear the disappearance of things he was wont to reverence without losing his reverence; let him

learn that he is here, *not to work but to be worked upon*; and that, though abyss open under abyss, and opinion displace opinion, all are at last contained in the Eternal Cause;—
   "If my bark sink, 't is to another sea."

(W, IV, 186; my emphasis)

The fact that "Montaigne; or, The Skeptic" should be present as signature and as subject matter in "Worship" signifies more than the telling irony that Emerson should choose "Worship" as the chapter in which to praise the rigors of skepticism. It further signifies Emerson's characteristic stance in *The Conduct of Life*, a stance that confirms power by affirming obstacles and that recognizes value by celebrating payment. Of course, these themes are given their greatest treatment in "Fate," the overture to the entire opus; and the fact that the famous peroration of "Fate" should be echoed in the peroration of "Worship" is ironic in the same way that the echo from "Montaigne" is ironic. For Emerson, the conduct of life, as well as *The Conduct of Life*, is now a matter as much of confirmation as of affirmation. In "Worship," the theme of doing as suffering, of action as reception, of devotion as patience, has been developed by iteration through some thirty-three paragraphs, covering some twenty-five pages of this second-longest of the nine chapters. Finally Emerson's antepenultimate paragraph releases his readers with an "And so," and Emerson proceeds to his peroration:

> And so I think that the last lesson of life, the choral song which rises from all elements and all angels, is a voluntary obedience, a necessitated freedom. Man is made of the same atoms as the world is, he shares the same impressions, predispositions and destiny. When his mind is illuminated, when his heart is kind, he throws himself joyfully into the sublime order, and does, with knowledge, what the stones do by structure. (W, VI, 240)

The question, Who should (or can) worship? can now be converted into the question that Emerson has spent the entire essay preparing by avoiding—What should be worshipped? Worship the Beautiful Necessity is his answer: How? By the same voluntary obedience that the essay on "Fate" has already, and more powerfully, sung.

The redundancy of "Worship" is extreme even for Emerson, and "Worship" is doubtless too long, in a number of ways, to be counted among Emerson's greatest essays. Its redundancy and lack of control do, however, serve to dramatize the essential problem of *The Conduct of Life* in a way that its greater version, "Fate," does not. "Worship" offers a dress-rehearsal of what it means—that is, what it costs—to experience the consequences of one's own insight, survive that experience, and live to recognize in its very difficulty a certain verification.

Cost as confirmation. "*Wass mich nicht umbringt macht mich stärker*" was to be Nietzsche's version, a metamelancholy conviction that may be paired with Emerson's own dictum, "We acquire the strength we have overcome" (W, VI, 255).[12] Confirmation is the assurance that, for worse as well as for better, desire becomes fact and perception is destiny. That is the theme of "Fate," the first and probably the greatest essay in *The Conduct of Life*. "Fate" investigates how perceptions and desires become actions, and how actions manifest their originating forces.

"Yet we can see that with the perception of truth is joined the desire that it shall prevail; that affection is essential to will" (W, VI, 28). The agent who lurks and hides behind the bland passive voice construction of that "is joined" turns out to be the perceiver himself. Characteristically, Emerson's claim here is at once more humble and more terrible than first appears. For, as "Fate" soon comes to declare, "Insight is not will, nor is affection will. Perception is cold, and goodness dies in wishes. . . . There must

12. It should be noted here that loss and victory are far from mutually exclusive for Emerson. Loss is often a form of victory, or at least a measure of victory, or at very least a sign that victory is still to come. In this paragraph from "Worship," for instance, loss is equated with calamity and calamity with the moral, the moral being itself a coin: "The moral equalizes all: enriches, empowers all. It is the coin which buys all, and which all find in their pocket. Under the whip of the driver, the slave shall feel his equality with saints and heroes. In the greatest destitution and calamity it surprises man with a feeling of elasticity which makes nothing of loss" (W, VI, 234).

be a fusion of these two to generate the energy of will. There can be no driving force except through the conversion of the man into his will, making him the will and the will him. And one may say boldly that no man has a right perception of any truth who has not been reacted on by it so as to be ready to be its martyr" (W, VI, 29–30). Confirmation is the assurance that perception and destiny are two sides of one coin; it is also the martyring process by which this assurance is sometimes achieved. The strength with which the house your spirit has built comes thereafter to confine you is the index of the strength of your building. The power that is obedience not dominion owes its mastery to a master; the master is Fate, which is one's truths (one's perceptions) become one's life (one's destiny).

When Emerson ends "Fate" with his famous hymn to the Beautiful Necessity, he is celebrating what I call confirmation. But before considering that famous passage in *The Conduct of Life*, recall that Emerson's essays are designed to empower rather than to instruct. John Jay Chapman describes perfectly the bracing effect Emerson's prose can have. A reader, says Chapman, "takes up Emerson tired and apathetic, but presently he feels himself growing heady and truculent, strengthened in his most inward vitality, surprised to find himself again master in his own house." [13] The remainder of this chapter is devoted to studying that state, for it is to the description and cultivation of that state—"the state of the votary"—that *The Conduct of Life* is ultimately dedicated.

EMERSON BEGINS "Fate" by announcing this fact. He does so with a diffidence that belies the importance and difficulty of the enterprise. I quote the entire first paragraph to demonstrate that diffidence, but also to reveal a combination of detachment and engagement that are easy to miss because Emerson assumes the deceptive, conversational posture of one on the brink instead of in the midst of his topic.

> It chanced during one winter a few years ago, that our cities were bent on discussing the theory of the Age. By an odd coin-

13. John Jay Chapman, *Emerson and Other Essays* (New York, 1898), 29.

cidence, four or five noted men were each reading a discourse
to the citizens of Boston or New York, on the Spirit of the
Times. It so happened that the subject had the same promi-
nence in some remarkable pamphlets and journals issued in
London in the same season. To me, however, the question of
the times resolved itself into a practical question of the conduct of life. How shall I live?

Notice that "It chanced" is Emerson's choice of an opening
clause for his essay on Fate, an essay he continued to tinker with
for some years after first delivering it in 1851.[14] The topic had
apocalyptic proportions and significances for him, as this wry
note to Carlyle reveals:

> I scribble always a little,—much less than formerly,—and I
> did within a year or eighteen months write a chapter on Fate,
> which,—if we all live long enough, that is, you, & I, & the
> chapter, I hope to send you in fair print. Comfort yourself—
> as you will—you will survive the reading,—& will be a sure
> proof that the nut is not cracked. For when we find out what
> Fate is, I suppose, the Sphinx & we are done for; and Sphinx,
> Oedipus, & world, ought, by good rights, to roll down the
> steep into the sea.[15]

Notice, too, that the second sentence begins, "By an odd coincidence" and the third, "It so happened." Not until the fourth sentence starts with "To me, however" do we get the counterpoise.
Even in this relaxed opening, the drama of the entire essay is

14. Owing to the increasingly disorganized state of Emerson's papers from
the years after his second trip abroad in 1848, no companion volumes to *The
Early Lectures of Ralph Waldo Emerson* (3 vols.; Belknap Press of Harvard University Press, 1959–1972) are as yet available. It is, thus, impossible to be as
certain as may prove important about the versions a given essay in *The Conduct
of Life* may have gone through prior to publication. Some chapters, perhaps "Illusions," may never have been delivered as lectures at all. Records of Emerson's
lecture engagements are unclear as to which lectures and how many constituted
the course referred to as *The Conduct of Life*, a course that is most often cited as
consisting of six lectures (when of course the book has nine chapters) and that in
any case includes various combinations of individual titles, when these are
itemized at all. See especially, William Charvat, *Emerson's American Lecture Engagements: A Chronological List* (New York, 1961).

15. Slater (ed.), *Correspondence*, 485.

microcosmically enacted. In the conflict between electing and accepting, desire and dictation, limitation and release, necessity and liberty, comparatively large scope will be given to the NOT-ME. When the ME finally enters, it will enter the more powerfully for having been withheld, and it will enter as perception.[16]

For if behavior, or conduct, is a language valuable for the risks of its readability, and if this concept of conduct is the central one in the entire book, the pervasive one is perception. How shall I live? means, How shall I conduct my life? and that means, How shall I read it? True reading is never, in Emerson, a reading of, but a reading through. It is always a question of transparency. As B. L. Packer has shown, such transparency is the apocalyptic achievement of aligning the axis of vision with the axis of things.[17] That coincidence of axes is achieved, or rather repeatedly attempted, through what Emerson calls "Use."

"The richest of all lords is Use," says a line from the motto poem to "Considerations by the Way." This use is not manipulation but internalization; it is not submission but appropriation; not aggrandizement but transformation. Use, then, is action of the ME upon the NOT-ME. It is thought resolving the beguiling but finally insupportable dualism presented by the medal of Jove. Such use is always that act of the mind called perception.

"The only path of escape known in all the Worlds of God," says "Worship," nearing its end and wearying of "the weight of the universe" it has been describing, "is performance" (W, VI, 240). That conviction seems inconsistent with "We are here not to do, but to let do; not to work, but to be worked upon." Emerson's sense of true doing, however, is a paradoxical blend of active and passive. Consequently, the apparent inconsistency is actually an acknowledgment that deeds, being of the maker not the made, belong to thought not to physical motion. Precisely this endlessly, or at least repeatedly, fascinating sum Emerson works

16. Compare Jonathan Bishop's analysis of Emerson's attitude toward circumstance and necessitated freedom, *Emerson on the Soul*, 208–11.

17. B. L. Packer, *Emerson's Fall: A New Interpretation of the Major Essays* (New York, 1982), 63–82.

from scratch in "Fate" as in all the essays of *The Conduct of Life*. The distinctive feature of "Fate" is its overt emphasis upon, and articulation of, perception as the concept that not only solves the sum but commits the arithmetician.

Numerous times, and each time surprisingly, the idea of perception functions to resolve a conceptual impasse in "Fate." Instead of detailing those resolutions I shall turn to the still deeper function of perception—its effect not upon the argument but upon the reader as coarguer. "The great day in the man is the birth of perception, which instantly throws him on the party of the Eternal" (J, IX, 217). What perception as a concept does for an Emersonian argument, perception as a capacity does for the Emersonian reader. It throws him on the party of the eternal; that is, it renders him of the maker not the made. This effect, Emerson characteristically avers, is instantaneous. Less obvious but equally certain is that it is not as lasting as it is instantaneous. Moreover this fleeting effect depends upon there having been a birth, and birth must be preceded by conception and labor. It seems, therefore, not too perverse or melancholy to see Emerson's faith in perception as a charge to the perceiver. Nor is it being more weighty than Emerson himself would wish to hold that Emerson's advocacy of perception succeeds as a charge, rather than lapsing into a piety, precisely because he arranges his essay to include the dramatic conception and the difficult labor that can bring about the birth.

The dramatic conception is effected by the union of opposites that Emerson keeps instituting. Instead of looking at the most imposing instances of such unions in "Fate," I have focused on the unobtrusive but telling instance constituted by the essay's four opening sentences. The obstacles Emerson then throws into the path of his argument yield their own strength to the reader who overcomes them. That strength is the strength to be a perceiver.

There are those who feel that such overcoming consists in dutifully reading all the way to the end of an Emerson essay. But I am speaking about the reader who feels that Chapman's description is the accurate one, the reader who feels strengthened in his inmost vitality. Like a spell or a charm, literature can evoke what it invokes. This may be especially applicable to transcendental literature, which, being always the literature of power, has, especially in Emerson at his most Orphic, deep kinships with the Dionysiac and the Shamanistic.[18] The reason Emerson can strengthen such a reader is that his essay creates that reader. It creates him the way any fiction creates its audience—by addressing him.[19] The rhapsodic peroration of "Fate" proceeds by a rather obvious direct address, that of the imperative—not the second person imperative, but the inclusive, first person imperative of shared activity: "Let us build" is the four-times-repeated injunction. It haunts as it compels, and imprints as it withdraws. The first person imperative includes the audience as capable of building even as it invites the audience to participate and even as it joins the audience to the speaker in common effort.

But this relatively flagrant means of evoking the audience has behind it a whole essay's worth of less-engaging address that nevertheless also functions to call into being the ears that are to hear. Although several of Emerson's perorations employ some bracing form of direct address (most often in the second person), and although many make a prophetic use of the future tense, his characteristic form is the declarative sentence in the present tense. Compared to the interrogative and imperative modes, and compared to the narrative past tense or the prophetic future tense, the declarative sentence in the present tense is, perhaps, the most aloof construction. One could argue that such sen-

18. Harold Bloom, "Emerson: The Glory and Sorrows of American Romanticism," *Virginia Quarterly Review*, 47 (Autumn, 1971), and Oscar W. Firkins, *Ralph Waldo Emerson* (Boston, 1915), 201: "There are savages who beat their deities; Emerson, clearly, is a member of their tribe."

19. See Booth, *The Rhetoric of Fiction*, 49–52, 363–64. The following analyses by Stanley Fish of the ways readers complete texts are useful in this context: *Surprised by Sin: The Reader in* Paradise Lost (New York and London, 1967); *Self-Consuming Artifacts* (Berkeley and Los Angeles, 1972); "Literature in the Reader: Affective Stylistics," *New Literary History*, 2 (Autumn, 1970), 123–62; "What Is Stylistics and Why Are They Saying Such Terrible Things About It?" in Seymour Chatman (ed.), *Approaches to Poetics* (New York and London, 1973), 109–52. For a program that calls for a literary history based on writers' changing conceptions and fictionalizations of their audiences, see Walter J. Ong, S.J., "The Writer's Audience Is Always a Fiction," PMLA, 90 (January, 1975), 9–21.

tences scarcely constitute address at all. But, like the lyric poem's declarative present, such sentences can create the more intimate relationship with their reader just because no specific relationship is posited. The hearer of such sentences is in the position that John Stuart Mill assigned to the reader of a lyric poem, the position of an overhearer. While it may of course encourage voyeuristic detachment from intimacy, being an overhearer can be experienced as intimacy bordering on identity. Whether, for a given reader, Emerson's declarative present tense actually fosters a lyrical alliance with the speaker or a detached, even disengaged, observation of the speaker depends more on the reader's proclivities than any maker of sentences can be asked to be responsible for. But that Emerson's declarative present *can* create such an alliance may at least be granted.

Further, the declarative present contains a third affective possibility in its very aloofness. Henry James described the aloofness I mean and attributed to it the paradoxical potentiality of involving the hearer: "Courteous and humane to the furthest possible point, to the point of an almost profligate surrender of his [Emerson's] attention, there was no familiarity in him, no personal avidity. . . . It was only because he was so deferential that he could be so detached; he had polished his aloofness till it reflected the image of his solicitor."[20]

If not from the intimacy of overhearing Emerson's declarative present, then from catching themselves reflected in its present detachment, readers may find themselves being created by Emerson's words. In "Fate" these words present for our individual and various response a description of "the huge, mixed instrumentalities" whereby fate is maker (W, VI, 8). The initial emphasis is on "mixed," for, like "Experience," the essay is scrupulous, almost laborious, about cataloguing the attacks that fate-as-circumstance makes upon us. Yet the emphasis comes to fall ultimately on "instrumentalities" because, although we are vulnerable to these attacks, Emerson acknowledges, we are not their victim.

In the polish of such aloofness we are, then, asked to see our-

20. Henry James, *Partial Portraits* (London and New York, 1919), 17.

selves not only as the golden impossibility that "Experience" tells us we are (W, III, 66, 69)—a dignity precarious enough in itself—but as the less noble though more vigorous creature that "Fate" and the rest of *The Conduct of Life* shows to us: "Man is not order of nature, sack and sack, belly and members, link in a chain, nor any ignominious baggage; but a stupendous antagonism, a dragging together of the poles of the Universe" (W, VI, 22). We are asked to see ourselves as a stupendous antagonism not the least of whose glories and sorrows[21] is to be attacked without being victimized. I know of no more costly confirmation than that one. That is, I know of no more difficult perceptual activity than that required to experience your own apparent victimization as, first, an example of nemesis whereby it is the attacker who is the true victim, and second, an example of compensation whereby the current expenditure *of* you is the means to an ultimate expenditure *for* you. "An expense of ends to means is fate;—organization tyrannizing over character" (W, VI, 8).

Shakespeare's definition of lust as "th' expense of spirit in a waste of shame" is not much more ruthlessly crude than this first definition of fate that Emerson offers. It is offered so that it may give way, twenty-three pages later, to "Fate . . . is a name for facts not yet passed under the fire of thought; for causes which are unpenetrated" (W, VI, 31). It is easy to underread that second definition and complacently decide that understanding makes undergoing possible. A more apocalyptic, more engaged, more dynamic realization and activity are, however, being called for and perhaps called forth. Penetration by the fire of thought must not merely allow survival; it must create capacity. This penetration by the fire of thought is a transcendent state in which the votary knows the earlier definition of fate to be as wasteful and wasting as lust. The votary has transcended the limiting conviction that fate is the antagonist of the self-as-maker. Instead, the votary experiences this antagonism as a strength to be acquired. To Emerson, it is precisely because we are such stupendous antagonisms that we can come to withstand, or rather incorporate, them. To invoke man as a stupendous antagonism is, for Emer-

21. To adapt the title of Bloom's essay.

son, to say of man—of all of us—what he said of his own style in
the dangerously famous letter to Carlyle that describes the results of Emerson's spasmodic efforts to compose as paragraphs
incompressible each sentence an infinitely repellent particle.[22] I
say dangerously famous because, as with Emerson's complaints
about his coldness, critics tend to take this description at face
value as a confession of organizational weakness. In fact, however, repellency is not a wholly negative quality to Emerson.
Writing in his journal four years before the letter to Carlyle, he
comforts, or perhaps only counsels, himself, "Every involuntary
repulsion that arises in your mind, give heed unto. It is the surface of a central truth" (JMN, IV, 325).

Like "Experience" and like many of the greatest parts of *The
Conduct of Life*, the whole of "Fate" can be read as a demonstration in which Emerson bravely heeds such repulsions and by such
bravery becomes able to see them as surfaces of central truth. For
Emerson, then, to attribute either to human beings, his audience,
or to his prose the characteristic of infinite repellency is for him
to do no less than characterize both in terms that indicate their
potential centrality. The state of perception that can change repellency into centrality, or transform stupendous antagonism—
however mixed—into huge instrumentality, is the state of perception that "Fate" is designed to create by exploring.

Curiously, Emerson's boldest articulation of what the requisite kind of thought entails occurs in "Wealth." He is at pains to
distinguish between the kinds of capacities required for physical
work and those required for thinking, and he is wholly unsenti-
mental—if appealingly rueful—about acknowledging that each
kind of activity "disqualifies its workman for the other's duties."
By way of illustration, he then adds, "An engraver, whose hands
must be of an exquisite delicacy of stroke, should not lay stone
walls. Sir David Brewster gives exact instructions for micro-
scopic observation. . . . How much more the seeker of abstract
truth, who needs periods of isolation and rapt concentration,
and almost a going out of the body to think!" (W, VI, 118). One
takes it that no less drastic or devoted a form of thinking than

22. Slater (ed.), *Correspondence*, 185.

this meditative kind is required to arrive at the state of perception which sees fate according to the later instead of the earlier definition.

The state to which "Fate" asks its readers to rise is a high one indeed. It would be foolish and offensive to claim that just reading "Fate"—even reading it very sympathetically—could enable one's thinking and raise one's perceptions to the requisite extent. And yet a start on that development is made, or at least offered, by the chance to grapple with the essay's infinitely repellent particles. For just to entertain openly such considerations as those in "Fate" is to have begun to create in oneself, albeit in the slightest degree, the wherewithal that may one day become the organs for such perception. Rudolf Steiner describes this phenomenon of knowing by venerating in the great opening chapter of his somewhat misleadingly entitled, *Knowledge of the Higher Worlds and Its Attainment*, which is the best book I know of concerning the kind of thinking Emerson alludes to in "Wealth" and the kind of perception all his sums and solutions call for. According to Emerson, "no man has a right perception of any truth who has not been reacted on by it so as to be ready to be its martyr" (W, VI, 30). Steiner is even more definite about the empowering effect of such committed perceiving; in a Coleridgean maxim, Steiner holds that "Every idea which does not become your ideal, slays a force in your soul; every idea which becomes your ideal, creates within you life-forces." [23]

Of course, one is left free not to be made in the essay's image, as one is left free by any work of art either to refuse to be its audience at all or to refuse to be as completely its audience as another might choose to be. It is up to readers how they will answer the question Emerson poses in this surprisingly late journal entry, from 1859:

A man finds out that there is somewhat in him that knows more than he does. Then he comes presently to the curious

23. Rudolf Steiner, *Knowledge of the Higher Worlds and Its Attainment* (London, 1963), 23. Compare Coleridge's "every object rightly seen unlocks a new faculty of the soul," which Emerson quotes in *Nature*, CW, I, 23.

question, Who's who? which of these two is really me? the one that knows more or the one that knows less: the little fellow or the big fellow. (J, IX, 190)

It is up to readers to decide whether the essay is addressing them as little fellow, as big fellow, or not at all. The reader who feels addressed as that fellow who knows more than the self is, however, the reader who can experience the surprising release of inner vitality and the restored mastery that Chapman speaks about.

The Conduct of Life not only pervades itself but surrounds itself with this theme of the requirements, costs, and results of perception. The repeated, various insistence on use as the richest lord of life is the book's way of pervading itself with the problem of perception. Its way of surrounding itself with the same problem is to begin with "Fate" and end with "Illusions." Such a framing is particularly suggestive in a book about conduct that defines conduct as perceptual capacity. To begin with fate and end with illusions is to begin with the deceptively implacable and to end with the implacably deceptive. Fate is inimical unless and until it is internalized, whereas illusions are dangerous only when they *are* internalized. Compare Northrop Frye's remark about the Greek *ananke*, or necessity: "It appears as external or antithetical necessity only after it has been violated as a condition of life, just as justice is the internal condition of an honest man, but the external antagonist of the criminal." [24] The truth, beauty, and goodness of necessity will always be obscured by the devastating illusion that fate is caprice. This pernicious possibility is the refrain of "Fate." "The secret of the world is the tie between person and event. Person makes event, and event person"; therefore, the misperception that keeps this secret is to think one's fate is "alien, because the copula are hidden." [25] But "the event is the

24. Northrop Frye, *Anatomy of Criticism* (New York, 1957), 210.
25. Compare this cruder version from "The Tragic," a lecture read in 1839: "And the first and highest conceivable element of tragedy in life is the belief in Fate or Destiny; that the Order of nature and events is constrained by a law not adapted to man nor man to that, but which holds on its way to the end, blessing him if his wishes chance to lie in the same course,—crushing him if his wishes lie contrary to it,—and careless whether it cheers or crushes him" (EL, III, 105).

print of your form. It fits you like your skin," and this truth will remain obstinately (or safely) hidden from one who submits to the belief that "events are arbitrary and independent of action" (W, VI, 39–40).

"Fate" defines this belief as the greatest, most disabling of all illusions. In doing so, it creates the space for a chapter on illusions, a chapter that may be expected to dispel illusions' necessary constancy as "Fate" dispels necessity's illusory caprice. Indeed, a journal entry from the year preceding the publication of *The Conduct of Life* speculates on the program for a piece that would neatly fill the apparent vacancy. "Were it not fit subject for poem, to send a soul to doom in the charge of an angel, and trace the angel's vain attempts to find a hell for it,—the assimilating energy of Osman converting every place into the one thing needful, and every hobgoblin into the best company!" (J, IX, 199). Surely such a poem could be a chapter entitled "Illusions." That chapter could crown with a hymn to use the book that had so carefully chronicled the various efficacies of use and that had begun with a hymn to the beauty of necessity which depended for its own beauty on the concept of use. But "Illusions" is no such chapter, and its final fable provides a totally different concluding note.

To be sure, it does deal in two kinds of illusions, those of the senses and the passions, which deceive, and those of the sentiment and intellect, which are "structural and beneficent" (W, VI, 319). Moreover, in conceding that not all illusions are deceptions, the chapter allows for the protective function of occultation whereby illusion accompanies fact in order to shield it from unworthy apprehension. But such resolutions and affirmations are not at the heart of this surprising final chapter of *The Conduct of Life*. Such a climax would no more befit the end of the book than it does the ends of the chapters. I have been arguing that those chapters begin in climax and end in initiative. The same is true for the end of the book as a whole. Its entire last chapter, like its ideal result, is ultimately initiative rather than conclusive.

The three features of "Illusions" that best characterize its entirety are its final fable, its ambivalent attitude toward its topic, and its surprising admission that "though the world exist from thought, thought is daunted in the presence of the world" (W, VI, 320). Indeed, that admission (or, as I shall argue, that costly confirmation) is the result of the ambivalent attitude and the source of the stark final fable; it is the ineradicable sign that this last chapter, unlike all the others, constitutes the capitulation of use to endurance. Emerson has postponed as long as he can the abdication of the richest lord, use, and he has done so so that endurance might worthily inherit rather than prematurely usurp its place. For in "Illusions," endurance, too, is of the maker not of the made. While in the motto poem endurance, the poem's last word, still has the character of a temporal capacity, that of stoic duration, by the end of "Illusions" its less temporal though still etymological meaning of hardness has been brought to the fore. This subtle transformation has been accomplished by giving free rein to an ambivalence that cannot be controlled, or cannot be otherwise controlled. "Horsed on the Proteus" of that ambivalence which now adores, now accurses the mutability that can be perceived only as obstructing illusions, only as the intricacy of the web never as the constancy of its design, Emerson uses "Illusions" to demonstrate what it will cost to live in a world that thought has created so well that it resists re-creation. Emerson uses "Illusions" to erase the entire book that preceded it, in order to make room for a new sum. In doing so he demonstrates his confidence in the possibility of finding and working such a sum, a confidence that it is difficult for his readers to emulate and therefore to credit.

Although Emerson's ambivalence about illusions is a metaphysical one, it is also, and more effectively, a psychological one. The metaphysical ambivalence can be resolved by reminting the medal of Jove so that illusions of the sentiment and intellect are structural and beneficent; only illusions of the senses and passions are deceptive. That is, metaphysically, Emerson can distinguish between illusion-singular as a beneficent principle and illusions-plural as dispensable tricks of the senses. But he is too much the poet to wish to extricate himself from illusions-plural, and too much the human being to be able to. Instead, he starts the demonstration of what he means by endurance by suffering himself to entitle his essay "Illusions"—plural, not singular. In keeping with that decision he then opens with a paragraph of apparent reminiscence that is almost frenetically paradoxical in its attempts to remain horsed on the Proteus of conflicting responses.

> Some years ago, in company with an agreeable party, I spent a long summer day in exploring the Mammoth Cave in Kentucky. We traversed, through spacious galleries affording a solid masonry foundation for the town and county overhead, the six or eight black miles from the mouth of the cavern to the innermost recess which tourists visit,—a niche or grotto made of one seamless stalactite, and called, I believe, Serena's Bower. I lost the light of one day. I saw high domes and bottomless pits; heard the voice of unseen waterfalls; paddled three quarters of a mile in the deep, Echo River, whose waters are peopled with the blind fish; crossed the streams "Lethe" and "Styx;" plied with music and guns the echoes in these alarming galleries; saw every form of stalagmite and stalactite in the sculptured and fretted chambers;—icicle, orange flower, acanthus, grapes and snowball. (W, VI, 309)

The spacious galleries of the cave are at the same time solid foundations for town and county overhead; the innermost recesses are a bower of bliss accessible to (and, presumably, captivating of) not pilgrims but tourists; with high domes go bottomless pits; the fish that "people" the waters of the river are blind, though—since their home is Echo River—it is not in any case their sight but their hearing that is needed. In this underworld complete with its classic boundaries that prevent any seepage between the consciousness after birth and that after death, guns and music avail equally to raise the alarms contained as echoes within its walls. To call those walls fretted as well as sculptured is surely to continue the *double-entendre* begun with "alarming," and to catalog the artificial vegetation of these walls' ornamentation by beginning with ice and ending with snow is to insist further upon the chill that accompanies the thrill of such a display. Clearly, the admirer of that cave feels an intruder; clearly, he is as much prisoner as perceiver of its fabulous attractions; clearly, the shortest sentence in that tortuous, ambiguous description is its most telling one: "I lost the light of one day."[26]

If the longer constructions record and enact an ambivalence that will not to be resolved by the essay's later progress, the shorter construction predicts the starkness of the fable that will conclude the essay. Indeed, in the tension between the ornate and the stark is to be found the true conflict of this deceptive essay. That conflict is not between truth and deception, as an essay entitled "Illusion" singular might have been permitted to be. It is not even between multiplicity and unity. In this essay unity cannot prevail over diversity by means of transformation, or use, or perception, for this essay has unhorsed use and put endurance in the saddle. Instead of offering unity by releasing the resolving power of use, this essay offers solace by affirming the irreducibility of solitude.

That this comfort is cold is predicted in the essay's opening and verified by the choice of snowstorms in the essay's closing fable. That this coldness is comfort depends upon two related, albeit mutually repellent, features of the essay—its rich, confusing ambivalence and its impoverished, inescapable starkness. These two find a momentary embodiment in the portrait of the sad-eyed boy whose lack of what the essay goes on to define as risibility sets him apart from the rest of the "joyous troop who give in to the charivari" (W, VI, 314). Surely that sad-eyed boy is a piece of self-caricature. Surely Emerson is here caricaturing his own aloofness, his own intense desire for withdrawal from multiplicity into unity. He caricatures it as an insufficient response, because an unsympathetic response, to life's rich show. Admittedly life's rich show is both mock and mocking, but responding unsympathetically is still unworthy. Emerson's self-caricature is

26. Compare Emerson's description of this trip in his August 5, 1850, letter to Carlyle, in Slater (ed.), *Correspondence*, 462. See also Slater, 469 and 470, n. 1.

an attempt to abdicate even the pursuit of perception in favor of the necessity of mere endurance. Moreover that caricature *is* caricature because it is the acknowledgment of a huge—if also grand—limitation.

In "Considerations by the Way," his charming and humble exercise in companionship upon the way, he has already conceded that the limitation is unavoidable: "Better, certainly, if we could secure the strength and fire which rude, passionate men bring into society, quite clear of their vices. But who dares draw out the linch-pin from the wagon-wheel?" (W, VI, 258). Who indeed? Not the speaker in "Illusions," not the author of *The Conduct of Life*. If it is a choice between a working wheel with linchpin and a useless wheel without, he will choose the linchpin. Without that aphoristic certainty but with the same indomitable faith in comedy, Emerson relegates the sad-eyed boy to caricature so that the reveling troops may continue to have their day. Yet he knows himself to be that sad-eyed boy, who can be deprived by illusions—however grand—of the light of one day, a loss for which the sight of stars during daylight hours is not a compensation. To lose a day is, for Emerson, to lose touch with the only source of vitality nature can give—her everlasting Now.[27]

"Illusions" is the testimony that even that source is caducous (W, III, 49), that even that god, once lost, is a half-god. Its final fable confirms that something remains, or perhaps only then arrives, when the necessary submission to the accursed and adored illusions has cost one the light of one day. Here is the familiar fable:

> There is no chance and no anarchy in the universe. All is system and gradation. Every god is there sitting in his sphere. The young mortal enters the hall of the firmament; there is he alone with them alone, they pouring on him benedictions and

27. See "Works and Days" (W, VII, 174) and the entire essay which, with its struggle to show time as an illusion, however "deep" (W, VI, 319), constitutes an illuminating comparison with "Illusions." See also F. O. Matthiessen's discussion of Emerson's poem, "Days," in his *American Renaissance* (New York, 1968), 59–64.

gifts, and beckoning him up to their thrones. On the instant, and incessantly, fall snow-storms of illusions. He fancies himself in a vast crowd which sways this way and that and whose movement and doings he must obey: he fancies himself poor, orphaned, insignificant. The mad crowd drives hither and thither, now furiously commanding this thing to be done, now that. What is he that he should resist their will, and think or act for himself? Every moment new changes and new showers of deceptions to baffle and distract him. And when, by and by, for an instant, the air clears and the cloud lifts a little, there are the gods still sitting around him on their thrones,—they alone with him alone. (W, VI, 325)

What arrives is the perception of oneself as the god one had thought illusions were obscuring. What arrives, then, is an experience of oneself as the ubiquitous center of a circumferenceless circle. Hardly a condition of Olympian conviviality, scarcely a state of ecstatic exaltation, this god-like condition is the grand alienation of the alone among the alone. It is that ultimate state of the votary, which "Worship" has already called home. Rhapsodizing on the power of the moral sentiment, that apocalyptic force stronger even than thought, "Worship" has prophesied that the "new church founded on moral science . . . shall send man home to his central solitude, shame these social supplicating manners, and make him know that much of the time he must have himself to his friend" (W, VI, 241). These lines are preceded by rhapsodic invocation of the choral song of voluntary obedience and necessitated freedom. Together the two concluding rhapsodies of "Worship" make a paradigm of the way "Fate" and "Illusions" surround, in all their mutual repellency, *The Conduct of Life*'s pervasive emphasis on use. They surround it with a call to worship the beautiful necessity and with a haunting answering call of companionship in the costly alienation that worship of necessity brings about, when it is successful. That grand alienation is not an estrangement, it is a solitude.

"'I join you, and leave you,'" says Melville's brilliant parody of Emerson, Mark Winsome, as he exits from a scene in *The Confidence Man* during which he has introduced the Cosmopolitan and Egbert to each other.[28] By means of the final fable of "Illusions," Emerson makes toward his audience the same paradoxical gesture of greeting and farewell; for with this fable Emerson joins us and leaves us. If he leaves us as truculent and inwardly strengthened as Chapman says he does, he achieves this by having joined us so variously, discreetly, and adroitly. He joins us to each other, to his book, to himself; leaves us to each other, to his book, to ourselves. Leaving his readers in their central solitude where they look at illusions while they are also being obscured by illusions, Emerson joins his readers in a shared poverty.

28. Herman Melville, *The Confidence Man: His Masquerade* (New York, 1964), 217.

II
Poverty as Adequate Desire: "Experience"

I now must change
Those Notes to tragic . . .
. . . .
If answerable style I can obtain
Of my Celestial Patroness, who deigns
Her nightly visitation unimplor'd
And dictates to me slumb'ring, or inspires
Easy my unpremeditated Verse . . .
(Milton, *Paradise Lost*)

The poet knows that he speaks adequately then only
when he speaks somewhat wildly . . . not with the
intellect used as an organ, but with the intellect
released from all service and suffered to take its
direction from its celestial life.
(Emerson, "The Poet," W, III, 27)

Heaven is so far of the Mind
That were the Mind dissolved—
The Site—of it—by Architect
Could not again be proved—
To Him of adequate desire
No further 'tis than Here—
(Emily Dickinson, Poem #370)

 HESE three passages provide two contrasting impressions of where poetic inspiration comes from. Whereas Milton's invocation belongs to a tradition in which poetry is granted from above and the poet is a supplicant or passive beneficiary, Emerson's and Dickinson's declarations place the source of poetry in the poet's abandon (Emerson), or in the poet's own desire (Dickinson). Since the Dickinson poem talks about Heaven and how its site might be reestablished, her idea that the mind's adequate desire would suffice need not, I

35

suppose, be considered as an idea about poetry and poetic inspiration at all. But the substitution or interpretation is warranted
by Dickinson's own familiar lines, where she not only puts poetry before Heaven but holds that poetry includes Heaven:

> I reckon—when I count at all—
> First—Poets—Then the Sun—
> Then Summer—Then the Heaven of God—
> And then—the List is done—
>
> But, looking back—the First so seems
> To Comprehend the Whole—
> The Others look a needless Show—
> So I write—Poets—All[1]

To return, then, to the contrast between Milton's prayerful reliance on his celestial patroness and the condition of willingness
described by Emerson's figure of release or Dickinson's of desire,
the contrast may be articulated as the difference between thinking of inspiration in terms of supply and thinking of it in terms of
need. Milton prays to be supplied, as hitherto, by the bounty and
good will of his celestial patroness, and he boasts that the wherewithal answerable to the demands of his "argument" comes not
from his worthless self but from "Her who brings it nightly to
my Ear" (Bk. IX, l. 47). Of course, Milton's topic in this invocation is the novelty and epic importance of his entire poem's subject matter—the fall into freedom; and Milton is concerned to
identify the demands of the new epic argument he wants his
poem both to initiate and to exemplify. Milton thus articulates
the standard his muse is to help him meet, but Emerson does not
specify what his poet's adequate speaking must be adequate *to*.
Similarly, submission to celestial direction is common to both,
but Emerson's involves a divine intoxication in contrast to Milton's blessed sleep. Consequently, though both Emerson and
Milton treat poetry and poetic inspiration as hallowed, Milton
imagines the poet being graciously and providentially supplied

1. Poem #569. Throughout, Dickinson's poems are cited by their numbers in
Thomas H. Johnson (ed.), *The Poems of Emily Dickinson* (Cambridge, Mass.,
1951).

so that the poet may discharge an elected task, whereas Emerson and Dickinson imagine a condition. (Dickinson's contrast to Milton differs in details, but clearly it is substantially the same as the Emersonian contrast.)

Both Emerson and Dickinson imagine a generating condition, a state of deprivation that is sacrificially induced in Emerson's case, painfully suffered or cultivated in Dickinson's. It is the condition of adequate desire that can generate adequate speaking. Though the phrase is Dickinson's the essentials of this concept of "adequate desire" are to be found in Emerson, who knew that value is risk and wealth is use and that new riches can come only to a suitable neediness. In "Experience" he dramatizes the implications of attaining, sustaining, or enduring this state. He says that felt loss not only confirms the existence of what is now absent but also intimates and enables its possible return.

"Experience" is probably Emerson's greatest essay. Rich and problematic in its claims and scruples, at once chilling and charming in its sincerity, it offers its face to its reader in a way analogous to that of its precursor, Montaigne's "Of Experience." In the idiosyncratic details of Montaigne's essay, you uncannily read yourself. Emerson's achievement is lesser, but similar: in "Experience" you read yourself not by that ultimate paradox of reflection whereby one man's idiosyncrasy becomes every man's quintessentiality (although Emerson is, of course, a tireless believer in the possibility and efficacy of such transformation), but by witnessing a reduction and being forced to acknowledge that the reduction is an exposure. The more Emerson takes away, the more precious is what remains. It is the sculptor's reduction— a carving away of the beautiful stone until only the statue and the empty, defining spaces around it remain. Reading Emerson's "Experience," one cannot presume to deplore the discarding of the stone and one cannot fear that the chisel is destroying instead of revealing.

The essay's organization is unusually schematic. Each of its seven parts is devoted to one of the "lords of life" whom the motto poem lists prospectively and the final section of the essay lists retrospectively as illusion, temperament, succession, surfaces, surprise, subjectiveness, and reality. But this ostensible explicitness belies the essay's subtlety. It is a complex of differentiating and relating, and it proceeds through an all but baffling variety of moods and tone. "I have set my heart on honesty in this chapter," Emerson confides (W, III, 69). Unashamedly he displays fear and hope, doubt and faith, enervation and invigoration, so that despite its schematic surface structure the essay's actual argument requires adroit attention. To read "Experience" requires not only suspension of disbelief but also of concurrence. In a curious way, it requires self-reliance rather than reliance upon Emerson, and for readers to muster such self-reliance is an effort. The difficulty of that effort is, in its own way, man-making, because the extent of our reliance upon Emerson measures the defect in our reliance upon ourselves. That is, if one is unable to forgive Emerson the findings of his honesty, what but one's own laxer honesty is to blame? What but one's own wishfulness feels that Emerson's realism is pessimism or that whenever he writes skeptically he must be abdicating?

"WHERE DO we find ourselves?" The essay's opening question is rich in ambiguities of tone and of reference. In tone it sounds as if it means, Where was I? Where, in the lifelong conversation with myself, did I leave off? That tone is a reader's clue to how to behave in the essay's presence. It is as though one is with Emerson in the study instead of being across a raised lectern from him; the seer is letting one see his fatigue equally without drama and without shame as befits this "sincerest of men."[2] Emerson's reader-listener is asked to perform the duties of an intimate: not to mistake what is painstaking for pain, not to mistake questioning for doubt, not to mistake hope for wishfulness. Only by performing these duties can you be an intimate of this essay, and the performance of the duties reveals you to yourself in a way that constitutes a special case of, if not a match for, Montaigne's demanding magic.

In addition to setting this tone for the essay, the opening ques-

2. Whicher, *Freedom and Fate*, 117.

tion can have at least two more meanings. It may mean, How does mankind locate itself in creation? Well, the solipsistic epigraph has said that we are nature's "darling" and are ourselves the creators of the very lords of life among whose legs we walk about dwarfed and "with puzzled look." Or the question may mean, Where, when one looks into oneself, does one find that which is truly the self? In its seven carefully separated and intricately interwoven parts, the essay will answer that a just and honest accounting of the power of spiritual law and the laws of spiritual power yields the characteristically initiative conclusion that Dickinson calls adequate desire. This *where* is a state that is, also characteristically, not a place but a condition. It is a condition of election marked by affliction. "Experience" explores this state of adequate desire and maps it as a group of principalities presided over by the lords of life. It is found to be the state of poetry, the condition of poetry, where condition means the *sine qua non*; and it is found to be characterized by loss—loss as forgetfulness, loss as separation, loss as deprivation, loss as incompleteness, loss as being lost. It is found, further, to be a state that cannot be inhabited except as a boundary is inhabited: with a persistent sense of homelessness, a chronic uncertainty, a constant sense of being deficient in something, the existence of which is verified by one's continuing hunger for it. "Narcotics cannot still the Tooth / That nibbles at the Soul" is how Dickinson distinguishes this poet's hunger from the hunger that is slakeable by religion or philosophy or science;[3] and it is Dickinson who describes the bitter glories of the precarious existence that is the only kind possible in this border region:

> Not probable—The barest Chance—
> A smile too few—a word too much
> And far from Heaven as the Rest—
> The Soul so close on Paradise—
> What if the Bird from journey far—
> Confused by Sweets—as Mortals—are—
> Forget the secret of His wing

3. Poem #501.

> And perish—but a Bough between—
> O, Groping feet—
> Oh Phantom Queen![4]

The threat that the poet-bird will "Forget the secret of His wing / And Perish—[with] but a Bough between" him and his paradise is the threat that the great opening paragraph of "Experience" identifies as lethe. By this lethe, "our life is not so much threatened as our perception." Lethe endangers the very quick, and it is the task of "Experience" to explore this endangered condition in search of the quick, so that its presence may be affirmed, its protection may be assured, and its power may be perceived if not released.

> Where do we find ourselves? In a series of which we do not know the extremes, and believe that it has none. We wake and find ourselves on a stair; there are stairs below us, which we seem to have ascended; there are stairs above us, many a one, which go upward and out of sight. But the Genius which according to the old belief stands at the door by which we enter, and gives us the lethe to drink, that we may tell no tales, mixed the cup too strongly, and we cannot shake off the lethargy now at noonday. Sleep lingers all our lifetime about our eyes as night hovers all day in the boughs of the fir-tree. All things swim and glitter. Our life is not so much threatened as our perception. Ghostlike we glide through nature, and should not know our place again. (W, III, 46)

This resonant opening chord answers both versions of its own question. Moreover, Emerson answers his own question by insisting on the principle of forgetfulness in a tone that should be listened to with that respectful forbearance I have tried to describe. Unquestionably, there is deep, even bitter, regret to be heard. Indeed, it must be heard out, for Emerson spends the first five pages of this essay repining the thoroughness with which lethe insulates from reality. It is lethe that prevents us from knowing both the scale and the direction of our doing. And it is

4. Poem #346.

lethe that is the "opium [which] is instilled into all disaster" with the caricaturing result that, "We may have the sphere for our cricket ball, but not a berry for our philosophy. Direct strokes she [*i.e.*, nature] never gave us power to make; all our blows glance, all our hits are accidents" (W, III, 49–50).

In "Experience" one *is* lost because one *has* lost. What one has lost is the power to make direct strokes. If it is right to hear bitterness and even resentment in the reverberating discontent that Emerson displays during the essay's opening pages, one can nevertheless hear also another note which, like a sympathetic vibration, sounds faintly but inevitably from another corner. That note is a redemptive one, of course, but its redemptive quality is less interesting than is the cost of acknowledging that it remains an overtone, rather than a note that can be struck directly. The hopelessness of knowing the value of one's work is offered as an early example of a lethe-besotted state: "If any of us knew what we were doing, or where we are going, then when we think we best know! We do not know to-day whether we are busy or idle. In times when we thought ourselves indolent, we have after-wards discovered that much was accomplished and much was begun in us" (W, III, 46). With this, compare "Illusions" on the same phenomenon, for "Illusions" supplies, as it were, words for the redemptive overtone in the "Experience" passage:

> We must work and affirm, but we have no guess of the value of what we say or do. The cloud is now as big as your hand, and now it covers a country. That story of Thor, who was set to drain the drinking-horn in Asgard and to wrestle with the old woman and to run with the runner Lok, and presently found that he had been drinking up the sea, and wrestling with Time, and racing with Thought,—describes us, who are contending, amid these seeming trifles, with the supreme energies of nature.
>
> ·
>
> If we weave a yard of tape in all humility and as well as we can, long hereafter we shall see it was not cotton tape at all but some galaxy which we braided, and that the threads were Time and Nature. (W, VI, 320–21)

Although the passage from "Illusions" may scarcely be needed to gloss the third sentence of the "Experience" passage, it does permit one to be certain that one is hearing what one thinks one is hearing in the terser version that "Experience" offers. Indeed, since "Experience" at its bitterest never fails to remember what "Fate" will come to call the beautiful necessity, and since "Experience" therefore is never far from remembering that there is compensation implicit in the deprivations it records, it may seem superfluous to insist upon the presence of this redemptive strain. My insistence, however, is not upon the redemption but upon the strain—what Newton Arvin calls, "the strenuous strain in Emerson's optimism."[5]

That strain is both costly and confirming. It is the cost that "Fate" will praise as confirmation, the compensation whereby the current expenditure *of* you is means to an ultimate expenditure *for* you. In "Experience" this costly confirmation is being examined from a closer vantage point; for "Experience" is being written *by* that expendable noncitizen, rather than *about* him. The difference is epitomized by another passage from "Experience" about loss as disorientation with respect to the value of one's actions: "The years teach much which the days never know. The persons who compose our company converse, and come and go, and design and execute many things, and somewhat comes of it all, but an unlooked-for result. The individual is always mistaken. . . . It turns out somewhat new and very unlike what he promised himself" (W, III, 69–70). In "Experience" Emerson attempts something as daring as the arrogant humility of Montaigne when he trusts that his idiosyncrasies will pertain to his readers. In "Experience" Emerson sets out to present reliable testimony from the mouth of the mistaken, failing individual about the unmistaken, unmistakably advancing All. It is as much a *tour de force* in tenacity as in honesty. As soon as you set your heart on honesty—which is to say, on aiming to make direct strokes—the first thing honesty reveals to you is the impossibility of making

5. Newton Arvin, "The House of Pain," in Milton R. Konvitz and Stephen E. Whicher (eds.), *Emerson: A Collection of Critical Essays* (Englewood Cliffs, N.J., 1962), 46–59.

those direct strokes. In the face of this stupendously antagonistic fact, the essayist can choose either silence or exemplification. That is, if one writes at all, one will have to write indirectly and call that indirection an example of the predicament that is one's subject matter. This, of course, is Emerson's choice, and it is to be noted that the choice is the poet's immemorial one, the choice of supremacy by fiction. If honesty's direction leads away from what it was hoped honesty might approach, then honesty's direction will be asserted and used as that indirection which can yet make the desired approach. It will be turned into ventriloquism, speaking from the belly through a dummy.

This orator's version of the poet's solution to the impasse places special burdens of performance on the orator, but it places at least as great a burden upon the audience—that of detecting and remembering that a role is being played; that of knowing the ventriloquist from his dummy even while enjoying the efficacy of his disguise. "Experience," like "Illusions," is among those essays for which there is no record of public delivery. It may seem curious that so oratorical a piece was never performed, but the peculiarity is less incongruous than it appears. For Emerson is an interior orator (and an orator of the interior), as Plato is an interior dialogist, not a designer of dialogue that is to be performed theatrically. (Significantly in this connection, Emerson says in the 1867 "Eloquence," "I believe that some orators go to the assembly as to a closet where to find their best thoughts" [W, VIII, 121].) Recognizing that oratory may be a less public genre for Emerson than one might have assumed helps to suggest that *interior oratory* may be as apt a term for Emerson's genre as *prose poetry*. I find the designation helpful because it takes into account both Emerson's persuasiveness and his aloofness, because it suits his lifelong preoccupation with eloquence, and because it honors his ancestral and regional connections with Puritan oratory. In any case, the device I am calling *ventriloquism* is Emerson's oratorical device for achieving indirection. Since ventriloquism can confuse as well as dramatize, I shall discuss two other instances of it in "Experience"—specifically in the sections on illusion and on temperament.

In order to give illusion, temperament, succession, and surfaces their due as lords of life, Emerson is at pains to establish the sovereignty of each in its principality. When, at the start of the last section of "Experience," he enumerates these and the other three in order, he calls them not only lords of life but "threads on the loom of time" (W, III, 83). This image of obscuring threads on a loom is at least as important to the essay as is the figure of the lords, for Emerson is less concerned with how much the commands of the lords of life hurt than with how much the threads hide. Indeed, like *Nature*, "Experience" is mistitled. *Nature* should be called *Man* or *Ecce Homo*, and "Experience" should be called "Perception" or even "Apperception," for in "Experience" Emerson is deeply concerned with the experience of evanescence. This concern is clearly demonstrated in the famous passage about the death of his son:

> In the death of my son, now more than two years ago, I seem to have lost a beautiful estate,—no more. I cannot get it nearer to me. If to-morrow I should be informed of the bankruptcy of my principal debtors, the loss of my property would be a great inconvenience to me, perhaps, for many years; but it would leave me as it found me,—neither better nor worse. So is it with this calamity; it does not touch me; something which I fancied was a part of me, which could not be torn away without tearing me nor enlarged without enriching me, falls off from me and leaves no scar. It was caducous. I grieve that grief can teach me nothing, nor carry me one step into real nature.[6]

Why, after all, does grief—even grief—make us idealists instead of realists? Not because Emerson did not deeply love and excruciatingly mourn little Waldo, but because his loss left "no scar." Not because illusion commands that it be impossible to feel grief keenly, but because, as a thread on the loom of time, illusion prevents one's bitterest grief from being sufficiently devastating to produce a revelation. The implication is dire: Truly

---

6. Bishop, *Emerson on the Soul*, 190–98, esp. 190. Bishop calls this passage a confession, but it is not a confession; it is a concession that the real is even more elusive and potent than the ideal.

(that is, directly) to perceive reality is to be not only scarred but devastated. As B. L. Packer has shown, Emerson conflates epiphany and apocalypse.[7] That is, what we survive must have been illusion, for death is the only "reality that will not dodge us."[8] The only true realist is a dead realist, for revelation must, by definition, annihilate him upon whom it is visited. As Emerson puts it in a discussion of truth, which may be the source of Dickinson's "My Life had stood—a Loaded Gun" (#754): "Truth indeed! We talk as if we had it, or sometimes said it, or knew anything about it. . . . 'T is a gun with a recoil which will knock down the most nimble artillerists, and therefore is never fired" (W, XII, 78).

Who speaks such hyperboles, Emerson or his dummy? Emerson is ventriloquizing, but he agrees with everything his dummy says. Moreover, Emerson, not the dummy, knows how to compute the import of what is said. "Experience" is an accounting; and its accounting proceeds by an arithmetic that is not of plusses and minuses, not of enumeration, not even of evaluation, but of use—use with respect to power. Emerson's ledger does not have "Experience" but "Perception" stamped on its cover; and inside it has, not debit and credit columns, but a single column headed "Power." The relationship of each of the lords of life to power is what Emerson is computing in order to formulate each as an entry in that column, and he knows what caution such sums require. The 1847 "Eloquence," in *Society and Solitude*, emphasizes the importance of exercising control over the complexities involved in this sort of computation. "There are all degrees of power and the least are interesting, but they must not be confounded" (W, VII, 74). Moreover, the essay goes on to take issue with Isocrates for holding "that the office of his art is to make the great small and the small great." Rather, Emerson holds that the orator must make "the great great and the small small."

To be sure, it is dangerous to put such persuasive words on the

7. Packer, *Emerson's Fall*, 57–63.
8. The journal passage on which this part of "Experience" is based adds, "If aught can act & react with energy on the Soul, this [*i.e.*, death] will." (JMN, VIII, 200–201).

supremacy of illusion into the mouth of one's dummy. But Emerson can afford to grant much because he claims much. In computing the relationship between power and illusion as the "Para coat" (W, III, 49) that makes us shed the very experiences we hoped were reality itself, he finds that by granting a shocking imperviousness to deepest grief he can claim an openness as yet unapproached. Despite his quickening always to the relatedness of things Emerson has a sure sense of level. It permits him here to claim (by implication, for the present) that adequate desire is harder to come by than the arithmetic of having and losing would suggest, and harder to experience than the pain of loss would seem to insure. By means of the risks of ventriloquistic excesses, then, Emerson has succeeded in "making the great great and the small small."

Though clearly a younger brother of illusion, temperament nevertheless has his own territory in this state of adequate desire that "Experience" is exploring. Temperament's speech on limitation begins with an image that harshly caricatures the master: "Temperament also enters fully into the system of illusions and shuts us in a prison of glass which we cannot see" (W, III, 51–52). Here transparency, that supreme goal of Emersonian striving, becomes the malignant effect of temperament. Through the action of lethe, life is a sleep and a forgetting; and, as though to insure impotence to your apperceptions, temperament—"the iron wire" on which the all-too-manifold and varicolored beads of life are strung (W, III, 50)—limits even what you can see because it encloses you in a prison house whose invisibility renders you oblivious of the limitation. If illusion-as-forgetfulness is a principle of loss, illusion-as-temperament is a principle of distortion, the more insidious for being transparent and therefore undetectable.

Unlike lethe, however, temperament is a power as well as a principle; and the self has power despite it—even, it seems, through it, if not over it. Since Emerson is careful to develop this point, it is unnecessary to read this section as mere defeatism. To be sure, there is no blinking the fact that temperament in as lowly a guise as a man's propensity to fall asleep in his chair, or giggle, or apologize, or overeat can render the endowment of "fortune or talent" worthless. To be sure, "men [may] resist the conclusion in the morning but adopt it as the evening wears on, that temper prevails over everything of time, place, and condition, and is [even] inconsumable in the flames of religion" (W, III, 52); temper is, further, proof against all but a few "modifications the moral sentiment avails to impose" so that "the individual texture holds its dominion, if not to bias judgment, yet to fix the measure of activity and of enjoyment." All this, however, is being said "from the platform of ordinary life" where "on its own level, or in view of nature, temperament is final" (W, III, 52, 54). Emerson has no need to reject this fact or to let it unbalance his assessment of temperament. As always he is able to "express the law as it is read from the platform of ordinary life," but also as it is read by his self-experience of it. And his self, he proceeds to assert, has experienced temperament as a limitation that cannot for all its force resist the "high powers" (W, III, 54).

In the first three-quarters of this section, Emerson has ventriloquized for his audience the speech on temperament as a physical scientist, a phrenologist, and a conscientious research assistant might make it. The performance is complete with scathing asides like "shall I preclude my future by taking a high seat and kindly adapting my conversation to the shape of heads?" Emerson does not mistake his *tour de force* for the real thing and neither should his readers.[9] Having put on his show and out-materialized the materialists who build "this trap of so-called sciences," he abandons ventriloquism, steps off the platform, and in fact dissolves the platform by asserting that on it "one lives in a sty of sensualism, and would soon come to suicide." But these talkers whom Emerson has been imitating and out-doing do not commit suicide. Why? Because, whether or not the possibility is acknowledged by them, "into every intelligence there is a door which is never closed, through which the creator passes." Against the bombast of materialism, "one whisper of

9. Compare R. A. Yoder, *Emerson and the Orphic Poet in America* (Berkeley, 1978), p. 48, n. 14.

these high powers" suffices to intervene "for our succor" and to awaken us "from ineffectual struggles with this nightmare," with this illusion that is temperament, enabling us to "hurl it into its own hell." There is no escaping Emerson's certainty on this frightening point. For him it is the irreducible spiritual fact.

Apparently, then, "adequate desire" is a condition which, though far harder to attain through even bitter loss or other keen sensation than the sufferer might hope, is nearer at hand than the prisoners in the transparent prison house of temperament may permit themselves to despair of. "No further 'tis than Here," Dickinson avers, and Emerson seems to agree. Proximity does not insure accessibility, but neither does unavailability preclude presence. The next section of "Experience," that concerning succession, ends with a clearer version of this certainty: "Like a bird which alights nowhere, but hops perpetually from bough to bough, is the Power which abides in no man and in no woman, but for a moment speaks from this one and for another moment from that one" (W, III, 58).[10]

LIKE THE other lords of life, succession has power to obscure reality but not to destroy it. The opening of the short section on succession reveals that Emerson is going to be more comfortable with this version of illusion, because he is seeing it as a secret and a necessity, seeing it, that is, as belonging more to the realm of cause and maker, less to the realm of effect and made. "The *secret* of the illusoriness is in the *necessity* of a succession of moods or objects" (W, III, 55; my emphasis). Nevertheless, this section, like the others, is being written not only *about* the expendability of the individual but *by* such an expendable individual. As a result, no matter how much he insists that "the party-colored wheel must revolve very fast to appear white," and that "in fine, whoever loses, we are always of the gaining party" (W, III, 57), it remains a strain to see confirmation of the general presence of power in the very absence of power from a given vessel, especially when that vessel is oneself.

10. The version of this sentence in JMN, VIII, 400, reads "*seems to me* the Power which abides" and "for a moment *seems to* speak" (my emphasis).

Emerson seems to avoid the strain during most of the section on succession, only to break under it at the outset of the central section on surfaces: "But what help from these miseries or pedantries: What help from thought? Life is not dialectics" (W, III, 58). This outburst measures how difficult it has been to speak— even ventriloquistically—as expendable noncitizen; but subtler signs of the difficulty are also to be found in the succession section proper. Compare, for instance, the following three passages. All deal with the expendability of individuals compared with the "vaster mind and will" which they but exemplify; all deal with the danger of mistaking vehicle for tenor. But the version from the succession section of "Experience" emphasizes the limitation far more than do the other two, not only ventriloquizing but, it seems, feeling keenly the deprivation of being oneself expendable and expended in this cause, however worthy.

First, this qualifying assertion about the uses of great men from the end of the chapter of that title which opens *Representative Men*:

> We have never come at the true and best benefit of any genius so long as we believe him an original force. In the moment when he ceases to help us as a cause, he begins to help us more as an effect. Then he appears as an exponent of a vaster mind and will. The opaque self becomes transparent with the light of the First Cause. (W, IV, 34)

Next, this fable from "Nominalist and Realist," a chapter in *Essays, Second Series* that provides numerous illuminating glosses upon the intricacies of "Experience":

> The magnetism which arranges tribes and races in one polarity is alone to be respected; the men are steel-filings. Yet, we unjustly select a particle, and say, 'O steel-filing number one! what prodigious virtues are these of thine! how constitutional to thee, and incommunicable!' Whilst we speak the loadstone is withdrawn; down falls our filing in a heap with the rest, and we continue our mummery to the wretched shaving. Let us go for universals; for the magnetism, not for the needles. (W, III, 228–29)

Lastly, the version of the problem from "Experience":

> A man is like a bit of Labrador spar, which has no lustre as you turn it in your hand until you come to a particular angle; then it shows deep and beautiful colors. There is no adaptation of universal applicability in men, but each has his special talent, and the mastery of successful men [note the pun on succession] consists in adroitly keeping themselves where and when that turn shall be oftenest to be practised. We do what we must, and call it by the best names we can. . . . I cannot recall any form of man who is not superfluous sometimes. (W, III, 57)

My purpose for pausing to quote at such length these passages that are difficult neither in themselves nor in their connection with one another is not just to emphasize individual expendability and the cost of relying on such—even such—a self. Rather, I want to indicate the special case of reliance and of self that this succession part of "Experience" adduces. Emerson opens this part of the essay by citing not anonymous great teachers as he had been doing in *Representative Men* before the passage quoted, not statesmen as he goes on to do after the "Nominalist and Realist" fable, but paintings, books, and the writers of books. Montaigne, Shakespeare, Plutarch, Plotinus, Bacon, Goethe, "even . . . Bettine," are named as the creators of books that, after they have provided Emerson with "tidings of their mood and some vague guess at the new fact," were fittingly dispensed with as having made themselves triumphantly obsolete.[11] It is Emerson's unshakeable position that strip-mining such Alps of the literary scene for their lustres is preferable to monumentalizing them because of their grandeur. Moreover, Emerson holds that precisely such reading is a verification that "while our love of the real draws us to permanence . . . health of body consists in circulation, and sanity of mind in variety or facility of

---

11. Compare "Poetry and Imagination" on the dispensability of the poet: "What we once admired as poetry has long since come to be a sound of tin pans. . . . Perhaps Homer and Milton will be tin pans yet. The poet should rejoice if he has taught us to despise his song; if he has so moved us as to lift us,—to open the eye of the intellect to see farther and better" (W, VIII, 69).

association" (W, III, 55). The trouble is that "this onward trick of nature" that is succession is lord over a territory in which Emerson himself pays a landowner's taxes. Surely the cost of being oneself expendable, not only as a man but as an artist in the worthy cause of general amelioration, is a cost that understandably induces anxiety in the artist who has elected to praise its confirming power.

"I would have my books read as I have read my favorite books," he writes in an 1841 journal entry, going on to emphasize that he wishes to be for his ideal reader not an "explosion & astonishment" but an "agreeable influence stealing like the scent of a flower or the sight of a new landscape on a traveller" (JMN, VIII, 106). Here in "Experience," Emerson faces what it would be like to have that wish fulfilled. His honesty tells him that the fulfillment of the wish will entail his being used by users; it also tells him that his wish is a just one because it follows from the truth that "Nominalist and Realist" opens by restating: "I cannot often enough say that a man is only a relative and representative nature" (W, III, 225). So be it, Emerson's gesture in this section of "Experience" seems to say—so be it, and I will be forgiven if I assert my belief with some distress at its personal consequences for me.

In his "American Scholar" and "Divinity School" addresses Emerson knew that being influenced by others was to be avoided, and in such later passages as these Emerson knows that being an influence upon others is a thankless prospect. Nevertheless, as R. A. Yoder has recently shown, Emersonian Orphism is a major tradition in American poetry, albeit a tradition which, as Harold Bloom has said, "can be called the only poetic influence that counsels against itself and against the idea of influence."[12] To continue this discussion of adequate desire, it will be useful now to turn to an important influence on "Experience" itself. I refer to Wordsworth's *Ode: Intimations of Immortality from Recollections of Early Childhood.*

In his own essay, "Immortality," Emerson calls the Great Ode

12. Yoder, *Emerson and the Orphic Poet, passim*, but especially the final part, "Legacy: Orpheus Descending"; and Bloom, "The Freshness of Transformation," in Levin (ed.), *Emerson: Prophecy, Metamorphosis, and Influence*, 132.

"the best modern essay on the subject" (W, VIII, 346). Emerson does so in the section of his essay that immediately precedes his famous dictum, "We cannot prove our faith by syllogisms":

> I think that one abstains from writing or printing on the immortality of the soul, because, when he comes to the end of his statement, the hungry eyes that run through it will close disappointed; the listeners say, That is not here which we desire;—and I shall be as much wronged by their hasty conclusions, as they feel themselves wronged by my omissions. I mean that I am a better believer, and all serious souls are better believers in the immortality, than we can give grounds for. The real evidence is too subtle, or is higher than we can write down in propositions, and therefore Wordsworth's Ode is the best modern essay on the subject. (W, VIII, 345–46)

Immortality is not a subject for questions and answers but for poetry. Indeed, "Of immortality the soul when well employed is incurious," says Emerson briskly in "Worship" (W, VI, 238–39); and it is not a concern with immortality that binds "Experience" to the Great Ode. Rather, it is the two works' contrasting attitudes toward forgetting and toward the connection between poetry and recollection that links them. Experimenting in his journal with the opening question of "Experience," Emerson seems to have associated it with Wordsworthian intimation: "Where do we find ourselves? In a series, of which we do not know the extremes, & believe it has none. We wake & find ourselves on a stair; there are stairs below us up which we seem to have come[;] there are stairs above us many a one, they go up to heaven 'Since neither now nor yesterday began / These thoughts which have been ever, nor yet can / A man be found who their first entrance knew.'" In "Experience" as printed, those Wordsworthian lines of verse (from Plutarch's "Of Common Conception against the Stoics," *Morals*, 1718, IV, 391) have been separated from the opening by some twenty-seven pages.[13] Into the gap have been poured those deluges of lethe that Emerson emphasizes in contrast to his precursor.

13. See JMN, VIII, 238, and note #117.

Whereas for Wordsworth "Our birth is *but* a sleep and a for-getting," "Experience" opens with emphasis upon lethe, deleting the "but" from Wordsworth's line. For Wordsworth, to see birth in this way is to experience an intimation of immortality as that which human beings have lost but which their poetry may re-trieve. Imprisoned in commonness, barred from glory and dream, one is doomed on earth to the sorrows and strains of a mediacy that is the redemptive residue, as are those "Thoughts that do often lie too deep for tears," of a plenitude of participation. That residue is a trace element, a vestige of former splendor. It is a relic that may be worshipped as the remnant of what once was and what the worshipper once was. Moreover, such worship stands to enable in the votary a compensatory capacity—the po-etic capacity, whereby,

> . . . the soul
> Remembering how she felt, but what she felt
> Remembering not, retains an obscure sense
> Of possible sublimity, whereto
> With growing faculties she doth aspire. . . .[14]

Emerson inverts the phenomenon of loss as forgetting and recollection as retrieval in a curious and characteristic way. For Emerson, it is not the past but the future that intimates our immortality. As early as 1827, at the age of twenty-three, he makes this entry in his journal: "If a man carefully examine his thoughts he will be surprised to find how much he lives in the future. His wellbeing is always ahead. Such a creature is probably immortal" (JMN, III, 76). The mock reassurance of "probably" anticipates that brisk, New England attitude toward morbidity on spiritual subjects that vents itself in Emerson's clear-headed denunciations of sensationalism in "Demonology" and that is again exhibited in "Worship." It also anticipates the sense that will become increasingly apparent in Emerson's work of how much such relentless reliance upon the future will cost. In 1845, Emerson writes a more effusive but also more searching version of the concept that a man's unmanifest greatness is inti-

14. Wordsworth, *Prelude*, II, 315–22.

mated by his being as yet unfinished, rather than by his having been reduced from a past grandeur.

> For the best part, I repeat, of every mind is not that which he knows, but that which hovers in gleams [,] suggestions [,] tantalizing [,] unpossessed before him. His firm recorded knowledge soon loses all interest for him. But this dancing chorus of thoughts & hopes is the quarry of his future, is his possibility, & teaches him that his man's life is of a ridiculous brevity & meanness, but that it is his first age & trial only of his young wings . . . that vast revolutions, migrations, & gyres on gyres in the celestial societies invite him [.] (JMN, IX, 341)

Significantly, this is the last paragraph of a passage entitled, *Influences*.[15] In this passage the influences are not those belonging to talent and ambition but those "more subtle and more high" influences emanating from the "friend whom we have not [yet] seen." That friend is a "leader"; he is "the Genius that shall marshal us the way that we were going."[16] Emerson's last sentence in the opening paragraph of the journal passage entitled *Influences* reads, "There is a vast residue [,] an open account ever." The residue that for Wordsworth is a mercifully unused portion of a vanished plenitude is for Emerson the as-yet-unused leaves of an account book still to be filled.

To Emerson, an intimation of immortality is not a past that is incompletely recoverable but a future that is incompletely realizable in a present. For instance, in contrast to the Great Ode's sense that maturity is what the departed glory of childhood has left behind, notice Emerson's use of the figure of the child in this passage from "Fate": "Whoever has had the experience of the moral sentiment cannot choose but believe in unlimited power. Each pulse from that heart is an oath [N.B., a promise] from the Most High. I know not what the word *sublime* means, if it be

15. Belatedly so entitled, judging by the insertion marks around the title as printed in JMN.

16. As the JMN notes record, this last clause (from Macbeth's dagger speech [II, i, 42]) is used in the opening chapter of *Representative Men* (W, IV, 25), a fact that is significant for the present argument.

not the intimations, in this infant, of a terrific force" (W, VI, 29; Emerson's emphasis). Moreover, just as defeat is for Emerson always the earmark of a victory to come, so even success, even realization of power, has initiative rather than climactic significance. "There is always room for a man of force," Emerson says in "Power," going on to say, "and he makes room for many" (W, VI, 58). Similarly, in an 1837 letter to Carlyle, citing his *The Diamond Necklace* for its "encyclopediacal allusion to all knowables, & the virtues and vices of [its] panoramic pages," Emerson continues with, "Well, it is your own; and it is English; and every word stands for somewhat; and it cheers and fortifies me. And what more can a man ask of his writing fellow-man? Why, all things; in as much as a good mind creates want at every stroke." [17]

One tires of this demanding optimism, this insatiable expectation, this too-adequate desire. One feels for Thoreau and even Webster when they are adjudged insufficient versions of their very selves, as Webster is in "Nominalist and Realist" ("Webster cannot do the work of Webster") and Thoreau is in "Experience": "We see young men who owe us a new world, so readily and lavishly they promise, but they never acquit the debt; they die young and dodge the account; or if they live they lose themselves in the crowd" (W, III, 51).[18] As a defining characteristic of the strenuous strain in Emersonian optimism, however, the wildness of being this ready to resume and yet again resume, combined with the serene acceptance of waiting that this wildness variously entails must be recognized (not to say suffered) by any faithful reader of Emerson.

Emerson's substitution of the future for the past as the measure of human greatness in no way protects him from feeling the present to be a state of deprivation. "Experience" must claim for the soul not the pedigree of having had a grand setting elsewhere but the predicament of being still about to rise in an elsewhere

17. Slater (ed.), *Correspondence*, 161.
18. See also JMN, VIII, 375, where Thoreau is identified by name in the sentences on which these lines from "Experience" are based. For the sentence about Webster, see W, III, 230.

that only the undisclosed future can locate. The forgetting that orients Wordsworth is the lethe that disorients Emerson. In an 1846 journal entry, he defines life as "the sleep of the soul."[19] And in the essay entitled "Memory," lethe is defined as, essentially, mortality, incarnation, experience—that which obstructs perception. "For the true river Lethe is the body of man, with its belly and uproar of appetite and mountains of indigestion and bad humors and quality of darkness" (W, XII, 107). That is to say, the true river Lethe is not located exclusively in Hades any more than the true God is located exclusively in Heaven. Both are located in human beings.

Lethe is a given for both Wordsworth and Emerson, but, whereas recollection of that which has been fragmented and obscured by lethe is possible for Wordsworth, it is not possible for Emerson. Robbed of immediacy, Wordsworth's mortals can move, however tragically, to mediacy.[20] But as Emerson sees it, we trope by default, not by privilege. Our troping is a mark of our poverty. Just as Emerson deletes the "but" from Wordsworth's sense of birth as but a sleep and a forgetting, he may be said to emphasize the "nur" in Goethe's "*Alles vergängliche / ist nur ein Gleichnis.*" For the Emerson of "Experience," you are not twice blest by a merciful correspondence between Heaven and earth, but twice cursed by an all-too-just correspondence that curses you by making you both giver and taker, both re-creator and exemplum of correspondence itself. To be sure, the difficult fact that man both tropes and is a trope can also delight Emerson because it offers possibilities for validation. "A happy symbol is a sort of evidence that your thought is just" (W, VIII, 13). In "Experience," however, Emerson is confirming the value of such correspondence by presenting its costs rather than affirming its pleasures.

19. The entry reads, "Life is the sleep of the soul: as soon as . . . a soul is tired, it looks out for a body as a bed; enters into a body in the season of dentition, & sleeps seventy years" (JMN, IX, 371).

20. On mediacy and immediacy in Wordsworth, see Geoffrey H. Hartman, *Wordsworth's Poetry: 1787–1814* (New Haven and London, 1964), 42 and the entire chapter entitled "Via Naturaliter Negativa"; see also, page 167 and the entire section, "Perception and Recollection."

THE SUBJECTIVENESS section of "Experience" figures the correspondence between transitory and timeless as a poverty. It turns
out to be a benign if "scandalous" poverty. For though "we cannot say too little of our constitutional necessity of seeing things
under private aspects, or saturated with our humors . . . yet . . .
that need makes in morals the capital virtue of self-trust. We
must hold hard to this poverty, however scandalous, and by
more vigorous self-recoveries, after the sallies of action, possess
our axis more firmly" (W, III, 81).[21] Why must we hold hard to
this poverty? Because it is the prerequisite for adequate desire. It
is the curse that says blessing must still be coming. This poverty
and blessing are, or rather is, the first of the Beatitudes: "Blessed
are the poor in spirit: for theirs is the kingdom of heaven." Such
poverty is not the genteel, Wordsworthian poverty of reduced
circumstances, but the crude, pioneering poverty of being as yet
without. Why is this poverty scandalous? Because it is a private
state which the public code has no way of honoring; we return to
it as the place for self-recovery after our sallies of action. In keeping with the economy of granting and claiming in "Experience,"
that word, *scandalous*, is both a wry admission of discomfort
and a grand call to perseverance, a wild cry of possibility.

This economy of granting and claiming becomes increasingly
intricate as the essay proceeds through the seven lords of life—
illusion, temperament, succession, surfaces, surprise, subjectiveness, and reality. "I dare not assume to give their order, but I
name them as I find them in my way," says Emerson (W, III,
83).[22] But there is a dramatic fitness in the fact that subjectiveness and reality are the last of the procession. Moreover, there is
definitive significance in their being least separable of all the
lords of life. Whereas Emerson treats each of the others in turn,
and although as "Experience" progresses it exhibits more and
more instances of enjambment—so that the section on surprise,

21. Michael Cowan, *City of the West: Emerson, America, and Urban Metaphor* (New Haven and London, 1967), 112–23, especially 121–23, comes to a
different but related conclusion about the value Emerson gives to subjectiveness.
22. Notice the double sense of "as I find them in my way," *i.e.*, "as they
come" and "as they impede me." Compare Cowan, *City of the West*, 112.

for example, begins before the one on surfaces is quite finished—
Emerson abandons even the semblances of category when he
comes to his last two lords. This change in the course of the essay
begins with its central section, surfaces. What went into surfaces
as forgetfulness and temperament comes out as reality and subjectiveness; what went in as succession comes out surprise. I do
not mean to be ruthlessly schematic (or wishfully so), but rather
to record that, as his essay progresses, Emerson deals increasingly with the affinities between and among the lords of life.

The penultimate section—on reality and subjectiveness—is
the essay's most difficult, because it is most wildly aphoristic and
most intensely compressed. Reality is the post-surfaces counterpart of forgetfulness; subjectiveness the post-surfaces counterpart of temperament. Taking these last two lords of life together,
Emerson sees their combined effects in the fall of man which he
opens the section by defining as "the discovery we have made
that we exist." [23] And the two *are* taken together, instead of being
treated discretely, precisely because our fallen condition demands
that our sense of reality be subject (my pun is intentional) to our
subjectiveness, and that our subjectiveness be proof against reality's universality.

It is easy to underestimate the gravity of this last risk, the risk
that one's very subjectivity may merge with, or be encroached
upon by, the subjectiveness of another, not by reality. For Emerson, socializing represented a danger to selfhood. His test for a
worthwhile social relation was exacting to the point of perversity. Every visit was an interruption unless it came from so kin-
dred a spirit that the visit could be called "a sort of joyful solitude" (W, II, 150). The penultimate section of "Experience" is
quite definite about the matter; for the lines about scandalous
poverty go on to emphasize the point by saying, "I have learned
that I cannot dispose of other people's facts; but I possess such a
key to my own as persuades me, against all their denials, that
they . . ." That they too can find a key to my facts? Not at all.
Rather, ". . . that they also have a key to theirs" (W, III, 81).

23. In keeping with the ensuing argument (Emerson's in the essay, and mine
here), what "is called the Fall of Man" is not the *fact* that we exist but the *discovery*, that is, the conscious experience of this fact.

Subjectiveness is the only valid reality; accordingly, its validity is not verified but threatened by attempts to share it.[24] The degree to which community threatens rather than supports this Emersonian subjectiveness is illustrated by the fable with which the paragraph in question continues. "A sympathetic person is placed in the dilemma of a swimmer among drowning men, who all catch at him, and if he give so much as a leg or a finger they will drown him" (W, III, 81). In short, scandalous poverty is the prerequisite of adequate desire, and that condition is lived out in solitude, albeit in the populous solitude of "Considerations by the Way." Using the same scene of drowning men, "Fate" underscores how populous that solitude may be, but how little help one possessor of his own facts can give to another: "I seemed in the height of a tempest to see men overboard struggling in the waves, and driven about here and there. They glanced intelligently at each other, but 't was little they could do for one another; 't was much if each could keep afloat alone. Well, they had a right to their eyebeams and all the rest was Fate" (W, VI, 19).[25]

Between the territories of these last two lords of life Emerson maps no clear borderline. The only thing that is certain about the principalities of subjectiveness and reality is that they do border and overlap each other and that, while anyone can live there, each one lives there alone. To live there alone is to live in a solipsism that is safe because it differs from insanity. Insane solipsism withdraws from the NOT-ME, saying, "Go away, you are not me." But this sane solipsism welcomes the NOT-ME, saying, "Come here to me for you are not yet me." The first is said by the mad solipsist, the second by the solipsistic poet—a tautological epithet as far as Emerson is concerned.

Since the dangers of solipsism are such an issue for British and American Romantics—from William Blake and his Ulro to Wallace Stevens and his "Rabbit as King of the Ghosts" or his striding singer at Key West—I pause a moment longer over the question of a benign solipsism. Consider Emerson's comparison

24. See the discussion of elective affinities in Chapter IV, herein.
25. Bishop, *Emerson on the Soul*, 209–10, interprets this passage very differently. He sees it as part of Emerson's capitulation to the idea that power is on the side of the NOT-ME.

between the solipsistic or imaginative Lear and the merely de-
ranged or fanciful Lear; and consider Emerson's preference for
the former—which who does not share? Emerson's comparison
bears on the distinction I am making, despite the difficulty that
Lear's being mad in both instances may seem to add:

> Lear, mad with his affliction, thinks every man who suffers
> must have like cause with his own. "What, have his daughters
> brought him to this pass?" But when, his attention being di-
> verted, his mind rests from this thought, he becomes fanciful
> with Tom, playing with the superficial resemblances of ob-
> jects. Bunyan, in pain for his soul, wrote Pilgrim's Progress;
> Quarles, after he was quite cool, wrote Emblems. ("Poetry
> and Imagination," W, VIII, 28)

I return now to the way Emerson relates reality and subjectiveness in "Experience." As Stephen Whicher points out, the
structure of this penultimate section of Emerson's essay "repeats
in abbreviated form that of the two chapters "Idealism" and
"Spirit" in *Nature*.[26] The reality of life is ideal because "life will
be imaged but it cannot be divided or doubled" (W, III, 78). Subjectivity is our only link with spirit because "the subject is the
receiver of Godhead, and at every comparison must feel his
being enhanced by that cryptic might. Though not in energy yet
by presence this magazine of substance cannot be otherwise than
felt" (W, III, 77). Whether one pursues Whicher's clue to make
the case that idealism "is" subjectiveness, and spirit "is" reality,
or whether one cross multiplies so that idealism and reality come
together on the one hand and spirit and subjectiveness on the
other, the similar structures of the two sets of meditations are
found to exist in both cases to support Emerson's central claim:
"Nature is made to conspire with Spirit to Emancipate us" (W, I,
50). To emancipate us from what? The more Emerson one reads,
the more inescapably one is forced to answer, from nature itself.[27] Emerson makes the point even more clearly in "Natural

26. Whicher, *Freedom and Fate*, 121.
27. Harold Bloom makes the same point in *The Ringers in the Tower* (Chicago, 1971), 223.

History of Intellect" when he declares flatly that "the senses minister to a mind they do not know" (W, XII, 37). Our estrangement from nature constitutes our poverty just as much as our fall from heaven does. Indeed, that is the ultimate scandal of the poverty that we must learn to hold hard to, and its ultimate use. Despite all nature's marvels and beauties, it cannot replace the heaven from which we have exiled ourselves. As the essay "Nature" has it, "Nature is loved by what is best in us. It is loved as the city of God, although, or rather because [,] there is no citizen" (W, III, 178).[28]

If in his first book Emerson comes to know this paradoxical principle of an emancipating conspiracy between spirit and nature—by getting drunk on its beguiling and repelling implications—in "Experience" he soberly assesses the cost of being the victim of this conspiracy in order to be its beneficiary. He assesses the necessity of the expenditure and finds it inescapable. He assesses the difficulty of paying it and finds it extreme. He assesses the value of the transaction and finds it all but inestimable. For, as the essay's final sentence proclaims, "The true romance which the world exists to realize [read "make real," not "become aware of"] will be the transformation of genius into practical power" (W, III, 86).

By the time "Experience" is ready to call them by name, "Experience" is not treating subjectiveness and reality as bars to perception. In their capacity as obscuring threads on the loom of time, subjectiveness and reality have already been treated; they have been treated as lethe and temperament—respectively, and also interchangeably. Their enormous power in that capacity has been vividly and scrupulously granted. Now a claim is being made about their necessity and about the beauty of that necessity. That beauty lies, as does all beauty for Emerson, in their relatedness. Far from being mutually exclusive, subjectiveness and reality are mutually enhancing. Reality is the goal of subjectiveness; subjectiveness is the use that turns reality into what it exists to become—"the true romance of the universe."

28. Compare *Ibid*, 190, and "Poetry and Imagination," W, VIII, 4.

This romance is to be distinguished from that false, lethe-riddled romance by whose dictates "every ship is a romantic object, except that we sail in" (W, III, 46). It is the startling, even stunning, feat of "Experience" to effect that distinction by transformation rather than by separation. What begins as envy for our neighbor's greener grass becomes, under Emerson's honest scrutiny, desire for one's own greenest grass. What begins as acknowledgment that "every roof is agreeable to the eye until it is lifted" comes, with the aid of Emerson's stern serenity, to be seen as that scandalous poverty that is the individual's only asset. Even the rallying cry of self to genius, "*In for a mill, in for a million*," which comes near the end of the essay (W, III, 83–84; Emerson's emphasis), has a counterpart in an earlier image. Near the start, Emerson likens the experience of feeling enervated to "millers on the lower levels of a stream . . . [who] fancy that the upper people must have raised their dams" because so little of the genius, so little apperceptive energy, seems available to them. The later rallying cry turns miller into mill. It turns a miller who was active and producing but benighted, into a mill, a tenth of a United States cent, which is to be risked even unto a million United States' dollars' worth. Call it dedication, call it acceptance, that last cry of self-reliance humbled into reliant self-risking turns the problem of knowing into the burden of being. The transformation of active miller into expendable coin is certainly a reduction, but it is not solely a diminution because the gamble in which the coin is to be expended represents, albeit only latently, wealth. The paradox that loss is gain because it makes room for gain is, for Emerson, an abiding complexity that is now terribly reassuring, now reassuringly terrible, but always to be reckoned with anew. "When half-gods go, the gods arrive."[29] Liberation by loss, compensation by survival, self-denial as self-reliance—all these are versions of the paradox and all are versions of costly confirmation.

I have tried to account for the greatness of "Experience" by describing and analyzing the various ways Emerson uses limita-

---

29. See "Give All to Love," W, IX, 92.

tion and reduction to effect expansion. These conversions constitute Emerson's confirming technique. They include surprising metamorphoses of the essay's opening images and concepts into its closing challenges and convictions. In the final lines of "Experience" the essay's very ventriloquism itself undergoes such a conversion, and I shall end this discussion of "Experience" with a speculation about that change. Throughout the essay, Emerson has been using ventriloquism as a means of recording the questions to which his claims have been answers, or as a means of granting all that must be granted before his claims will stand out in the stark relief proper to them. That is, until he comes to the end of "Experience" Emerson uses ventriloquism for what he will not say, though it must be said. Now, at the end of the essay, Emerson would say that which he cannot yet say; he would give counsel, courage, hope that he is too depleted to give in his own person. Honesty forces him to disqualify himself as the person who can speak the essay's closing challenge, because his calculations concerning the accessibility of power to a given insolvent noncitizen have led him to acknowledge, "All I know is reception; I am and I have; but I do not get" (W, III, 83). "I do not get" means, I do not beget, so that the assertion is a compound of claiming and granting, and its comfort depends at least as much upon acceptance of stricture as it does upon hope for release. Precisely this quality of offering the very strenuousness of hope as its most reliable and realistic feature, because its irreducible feature is the quality that constitutes the strength and appeal of "Experience." But, bracing as such companionship in strain may be, it leaves Emerson too much a member of his own audience to permit him to remain the exhorter who offers the final charge that is now needed. Instead of Emerson, who does speak this final charge? "Never mind the ridicule, never mind the defeat; up again old heart!—it seems to say,—there is victory yet for all justice; and the true romance which the world exists to realize will be the transformation of genius into practical power" (W, III, 85–86).

Who or what is the "it" who "seems to say" this comforting challenge, or challenging comfort? The context is not much help in assigning the proper antecedent, for the preceding sentence reads, "We dress our gardens, eat our dinners, discuss the household with our wives, and these things make no impression, are forgotten next week; but, in the solitude to which every man is always returning, he has a sanity and revelations which in his passage into new worlds he will carry with him" (W, III, 85). That is, the "it" must refer to a noun from the second half of this sentence—the part after the semicolon. "It" must be either the "solitude to which every man is always returning" (though this solution posits an unlikely personification), or—despite the agreement problem—"it" must be the "sanity and revelations" which that solitude vouchsafes and protects. My own solution is that the "it" who speaks this closing charge in "Experience" is *Nature*'s Orphic poet.

Just as Emerson cannot end *Nature* in his own person, but prefers to assign the supreme "traditions of man and nature" to a fiction (W, I, 70), so Emerson cannot say what he would say in "Experience." Such assignments of wisdom and encouragement to a displaced, sublimated speaker could be read as revealing that Emerson lacks confidence in the comfort and challenge he offers. And I do read them as disclaimers, in both *Nature* and "Experience." But it is the right to speak that Emerson seems to be disclaiming, rather than the rightness of what is being spoken. It is true that *Nature* identifies its final speaker by trade if not by name and, moreover, reinforces the impression of recorded speech by using quotation marks around the Orphic poet's paragraphs. It is true that in "Experience," the closing Orphic charge—though equally vatic—represents a reduction in everything from discursiveness to grandeur of persona, as befits the more sober tone of the essay. Nevertheless, for Emerson to assign the closing challenges of both *Nature* and "Experience" to another speaker suggests to me that Emerson has moved from his position as speaker and ventriloquizer into the position of listener. With that move, Emerson enacts that he, no less than any member of his audience, is "too young yet by some ages to compile a code" that will reveal order and unity where there now is lethe and fragmentation (W, III, 83). Meantime, Emerson can wait.

In order to lay claim to this youth, Emerson must disassociate himself from the egotistical sublime in which both Wordsworth and Montaigne have preceded and bested him. He must choose instead what is left—a severely limited kind of negative capability. This is not the negative capability that is the poet's protean ability to be, in order to see and to say; ventriloquizing had been Emerson's version of this. Now the stress must be on the negative, as distinct from the capability. Emerson becomes a listener instead of a speaker. The gesture is related to the one that closes "Illusions" and thus all of *The Conduct of Life*. With it, Emerson makes room for the possible arrival of the gods by renouncing speech and choosing listening instead. In "Experience" Emerson's adroit impersonations and his final conversion from speaker to listener are part of the granting and claiming by which the essay proceeds. Emerson puts that same facility to other uses, too. Attending to some of these local effects of Emerson's rhetorical art will provide further opportunity to observe Emerson's confirming technique.

III
Leasts and Lustres:
Emerson's Fables

> *In fact, Emerson is an essence, a condensation; more so, perhaps, than any other man who has appeared in literature. Nowhere else is there such a preponderance of pure statement, of the very attar of thought over the bulkier, circumstantial, qualifying or secondary elements. He gives us net results.* (John Burroughs, *Birds and Poets*)

> *I think, in the higher societies of the Universe, it will turn out, that the angels are molecules, as the devils were always Titans, since the dulness of the world needs such mountainous demonstrations, & the virtue is so modest & concentrating.* (Emerson to Carlyle, April 29, 1843)

> *I read for the lustres.* (Emerson, "Experience," W, III, 233)

 S THE three epigraphs to this chapter suggest, condensation may function as a kind of expansion or as a means to expansion. The paradoxical relationship between condensation and expansion deeply interested and reassured Emerson. He mistrusted bulk, trusted the telling detail, and particularly valued what he called "the delicious sense of indeterminate size" (W, IV, 17).[1] The transcendent sense

---

1. R. A. Yoder discusses Emerson's tendency to miniaturize as it appears in Emerson's poems and as it influences his Orphic descendants. See Yoder, "Toward the 'Titmouse Dimension'," 255–70, and Yoder, *Emerson and the Orphic Poet*, 134–205. Yoder's ideas about the titmouse dimension and mine about Emerson's fables are similar, but whereas Yoder sees Emerson's perceptions and productions in the titmouse dimension as effective strategic retrenchment, I see Emerson's faith in fables and use of them as confirmations. What Yoder sees as an honorable and influential prudence or stoicism I see as a quiet and forceful intensification.

of feeling not so much large as boundless always announced to him, and heralds in his essays, that fluidity of consciousness and adaptibility of thinking which would permit perception and articulation where before there had been resistance and bafflement. When the imagination wakes, he writes in the opening chapter of *Representative Men*, "a man seems to multiply ten times or a hundred times his force. It opens the delicious sense of indeterminate size and inspires an audacious mental habit. We are . . . elastic . . . and a sentence in a book, or a word dropped in conversation, sets free our fancy, and instantly our heads are bathed with galaxies, and our feet tread the floor of the Pit. . . . And once having passed the bounds, [we] shall never again be quite the miserable pedants we were" (W, IV, 17).[2]

What Emerson called "leasts" perennially fascinated him because they could give the sense of indeterminate size. Leasts were microcosms and they were also minute differences with large consequences as this passage from "Works and Days" reflects:

> 'T is the very principle of science that Nature shows herself best in leasts; it was the maxim of Aristotle and Lucretius; and, in modern times, of Swedenborg and Hahnemann.[3] The order of changes in the egg determines the age of fossil strata. So it was the rule of our poets . . . that the fairies largest in power were the least in size. In the Christian graces, humility stands highest of all, in the form of the Madonna; and in life, this is the secret of the wise. We owe to Genius always the same debt, of lifting the curtain from the common, and showing us that divinities are sitting disguised in the seeming gang of gypsies and pedlers. (W, VII, 176)

Here Emerson begins by defining leasts as microcosms and therefore as correspondences or tropes: a single cell's development can stand as the analogy for epochs of evolution. But as the passage continues, Emerson shifts from describing leasts as analogies to considering leasts as degrees or differences. Starting with

2. See also W, VIII, 18.
3. Christian Friedrich Samuel Hahnemann, 1755–1843, founder of homeopathic medicine.

the reference to fairies and culminating in the curtain image, his conception of leasts changes until they become surprising differences as well as revealed similarities. Such critical hairs of separation fascinate Emerson because they present to his belief in correspondence the vitalizing obstacle of a recognition of dissimilarity. That is, they offer the enduring puzzle of when a difference in degree becomes a difference in kind.

In the temperament section of "Experience" Emerson dramatizes that puzzle in a revealing way. "Spirit is matter reduced to an extreme thinness: O *so* thin!" (W, III, 53; Emerson's emphasis). With this ventriloquized assertion Emerson renders the impudent knowingness of those physicians who wish to assure all comers that they are not materialists but idealists. Only presumptuous fools think that spirit is just rarefied matter. They betray their ignorance precisely when they presume that it is spirit that depends upon matter. Exposing the blunder and disposing of it, Emerson continues—now in his own voice: "But the definition of *spiritual* should be, *that which is its own evidence*" (W, III, 53; Emerson's emphasis).

If the definition of spirit is that which is its own evidence, an important characteristic of spirit is its tendency to eventuate in words, deeds, or things. Emerson's idea of "Man [as] that noble endogenous plant which grows, like the palm, from within outward" (W, IV, 6), may be taken also as his idea of this definitive property of spirit—its tendency to articulation. Thus, though spirit does not depend on matter, spirit and matter are vitally related. Spirit tends to manifest. In matter, spirit creates leasts—confining yet confirming articulations of itself. The vignettes, anecdotes, and fables that proliferate in Emerson's prose function similarly. They contain and then release the infinitude that he designed every essay to proclaim.

Always mindful that the rhapsodic and the definitive were competing modes, Emerson was avid to make suggestion mediate between Orphic pronouncement and prosaic statement, between vision proclaimed and vision reported, or between the releasing wildness of interior oratory and the constricting persuasiveness of declaimed oratory. As a result, Emerson continually sought utterance that could accommodate. He sought ways to preserve the radical distinction between spirit and matter and yet *use* the distinction as that "internal difference / Where the meanings are" which Emily Dickinson knew so well. "Fable," he wrote in an 1835 journal entry, "avoids the difficulty, is at once exoteric & esoteric, & is clapped by both sides" (JMN, V, 31). Because of unrecoverable erasures on the journal page it is impossible to know what "the difficulty" refers to. Even so, it seems clear that fables are being valued for their accommodation of conflicting expectations, demands, or needs. Moreover, under the subheading "Veracity" in "Poetry and Imagination," Emerson stresses the necessity for accommodation in similar terms: "All writings must be in a degree exoteric, written to a human *should* or *would*, instead of to the fatal *is*: this holds even of the bravest and sincerest of writers" (W, VIII, 30–31; Emerson's emphasis). (Parenthetically it should be noted that for Emerson the distinction is not between should and would but between should-or-would and is. To note this is to remember that Emerson is not a moralizer about sentiment, but a poet of the moral sentiment.)

In order to effect a correspondence between the esoteric ("fatal") *is* and the exoteric ("human") *should* or *would*, Emerson uses the overt fable as parable or as analogy. Fable may be addressed to both one's audiences: the townspeople gathered in the lyceum for the entertainment and edification to which their tickets entitle them and that other audience which Emerson defines as those "few intelligent persons whom the writer believes to exist in the millions" and to whom "every book is written with a constant secret reference" (W, VIII, 219).

Compared to the relatively esoteric message it conveys, the fable is, for Emerson, a thing. When argument can eventuate in such a thing it has revealed its spirituality by manifesting itself as fable, as relative matter, as medium for essentially mediumless message. An 1847 journal passage puts it more plainly: "America is formless, has no terrible and no beautiful condensation. Genius always anthropomorphist, runs every idea into a fable, constructs, finishes, as the plastic Italian cannot build a post or a pumphandle but it terminates in a human head" (JMN, X, 80).[4] To Emerson the value of a fable is that of any trope: its analogizing force is epiphanic.[5] The particular value of fables as tropes is that their invention is a form of discovery; or to put it another way, fables are especially graphic instances of the fact that originality is quotation.

Lawrence Buell notices an anecdotal tendency in the later Emerson and deplores it as a displacement of a carefully exploited and programmatically symbolic earlier use of the "exemplary I" by a self-indulgent, inadvertent personal I. Buell does grant that the "voice of private opinion" and Emerson's "increasing tendency to speak off the top of his head" have versions in *Representative Men* and later volumes that are "still a long way from the cozy, crotchety old scholar that one finds in 'Books.'"[6] Consequently Buell might well agree that the particular touches of informality I am discussing function as vitally as I am arguing they do. Nevertheless Buell associates this less formal mode with that falling off that every critic of Emerson has attested to.

Earlier reference was made to the chiding solicitousness with which readers regarded the unfolding of Emerson's work, and to his own familiarity with that solicitousness as reflected in this journal entry from the winter of 1850: "The fate of my books is like the impression of my face. My acquaintances, as long back as I can remember, have always said, 'Seems to me you look a little thinner than when I saw you last'" (JMN, XI, 214). Curiously and usefully, the image of the face is used by the naturalist John Burroughs in his appreciation of Emerson:

Everything about a man like Emerson is important. I find his

4. See also Henry David Thoreau's long passage on the efficacies of fable, which begins: "The fable which is naturally and truly composed, so as to satisfy the imagination ere it addresses the understanding . . . is to the wise man an apothegm, and admits of his most generous interpretation." *A Week on the Concord and Merrimack Rivers, Works* (Boston and New York, 1906), I, 58ff.

5. See W, VIII, 13, and Chapter II, note 22, herein. See also "The Poet" (W, III, 15–33 and *passim*), especially p. 31, where Emerson says that the analogies poets find are liberating because they give "a cheerful hint of the immortality of our essence and its versatile habit and escapes."

6. Buell, *Literary Transcendentalism*, 284–96.

phrenology and physiognomy more than ordinarily typical and suggestive. Look at his picture there—large strong features on a small face and head—no blank spaces; all given up to expression. . . . In most men there is more face than feature, but here is a vast deal more feature than face, and a corresponding alertness and emphasis of character.[7]

One suspects that Emerson would have liked the saving way Burroughs divides the word *face* into the concepts of face and feature, so that thinness of face may mean sharpness of feature rather than reduction of strength. Later Burroughs finds another way to concede thinness without having to assume weakness. "His power of statement is enormous; his scope of being is not enormous."[8] This power of statement has its source in two qualities of Emerson's mind for which Burroughs finds just the right images:

His mind has the hand's pronounced anatomy, its cords and sinews and multiform articulations and processes, its opposing and coordinating power. . . . Where he is at all he is entirely—nothing extemporaneous; his most casual word seems to have laid in pickle a long time, and is saturated through and through with the Emersonian brine. Indeed so pungent and penetrating is his quality, that even his quotations seem more than half his own.[9]

About the prehensile quality of Emerson's mind enough has been said, in this study and in numerous others. But Burroughs' remarks about the pungency of Emerson's most casual word bear further examination in connection with Emerson's leasts as lustres. Consider one passage that demonstrates the accuracy of Burroughs' figure about words pickled in brine, and then one that demonstrates how serious a quality Burroughs' figure identifies.

In his address at Thoreau's funeral Emerson shared an anecdote about a descriptive utterance made by a "friend" of Thoreau

7. John Burroughs, "Emerson," *Birds and Poets* (Boston and New York, 1891), 190.
8. *Ibid.*, 197.
9. *Ibid.*, 191.

who was, in fact, Emerson himself: "'I love Henry,' said one of his friends, 'but I cannot like him; and as for taking his arm, I should as soon think of taking the arm of an elm-tree'" (W, X, 456). Edward Emerson's note tells us that Emerson himself was the friend who made this revealing and now famous remark, but the note does not tell whether Emerson intentionally or unintentionally disguised himself in this instance. If intentionally, then he is proliferating versions of himself. If unintentionally, then Emerson is so thoroughly saturated with the brine of his own utterance that he is actually unaware that he himself is the source of the witticism he admires!

This saturation or readiness that Burroughs so aptly identified and characterized becomes a serious topic in a passage from the 1867 "Eloquence." In the passage Emerson permits himself an historical anecdote that does not have his usual detachment. The anecdote is at the expense of Charles Chauncy who, though an eminent clergyman, found himself at a loss for words when he was asked to pray extemporaneously for "a little boy [who] had fallen into Frog Pond on the Common and was drowned." Emerson writes, "The doctor [*i.e.*, Chauncy] was much distressed, and in his prayer he hesitated. . . . He prayed for Harvard College, he prayed for the schools, he implored the Divine Being 'to—to—bless to them all the boy that was this morning drowned in Frog Pond'" (W, VIII, 127). Emerson sternly goes on to say, "Now this is not want of talent or learning, but of manliness," by which, it is clear, he means that readiness which he finds to be the fundamental principle of all eloquence (as both the 1847 and 1867 essays of that title propound). Though spontaneity is the readiness poor Chauncy lacks, and though Emerson constantly repined that lack in himself, a more reliable if harder-won readiness could also serve. With the aid of Burroughs' image and insight we may distinguish between spontaneity and such readiness. It is the readiness achieved by long steeping in the same few ideas, the readiness achieved as habit if it could not be achieved as inspiration. This kind of readiness was, of course, Emerson's.

As the Chauncy anecdote implies, readiness is possible only because the common and the elevated are one. When readiness is not present in a speaker, this must mean that the speaker has severed the common from the elevated. It must mean that as surely as he went up by the pulpit stairs he went away from the boy at the bottom of Frog Pond. The boy is "on the Common"; if the speaker is not, he is ineloquent, undivine, unhuman. To make certain of scoring this point, Emerson does not scruple to catch Chauncy at an all too apt private prayer as well as at his inept public one. "I should add what is told of him . . . that he had once prayed that 'he might never be eloquent'; and, it appears, his prayer was granted" (W, VIII, 128). Nothing angered Emerson more than the ultimate breach in manners constituted by a breach in eloquence; and nothing was dearer to his heart than the readiness true eloquence depended upon.

Whatever other attributes he may have, Emerson's ideal man, to whom he referred by the name Osman, is, by the etymology of his name, a man of bone (*os, ossis*), or perhaps of the face or mouth (*ōs, ōris*), or—most probably—both. Osman figures only once in the essays, in a parable near the end of "Manners" (W, III, 154). But journal references to him are quite common though often cryptic. In any case, speculation about the etymological fitness of his name is suggested by, and suggestive of, Emerson's anthropomorphizing means to utterance. As befits those of an interior orator, these are not so much persuasive means as they are plasticizing means. That is, while Emerson's anecdotal characters are personae, these personae are instances more than they are strategies, suggestions more than identifications, experimental *dis*placements more than definitive placements. "When a god wishes to ride, any chip or pebble will bud and shoot out winged feet and serve him for a horse" (W, VI, 48). This is the secret motto of the confirming Emerson. If his argument is sufficiently godlike, if he achieves real eloquence, then the mark of that achievement will be that his rhetorical chips and pebbles will "bud and shoot out winged feet" and will serve as sufficient vehicle.

WE HAVE seen that behavior is language for Emerson, and best behavior is eloquence. And we have seen that Emerson is preeminently an interior orator and therefore not primarily concerned with the techniques or dynamics of persuasion; rather, he is concerned with speech as utterance, as externalization, as outer-ing. If the important characteristic of spirit is, for all practical purposes, that it eventuate in a thing, then speaking, the chief event or activity by which this outering is achieved, is of sublime importance. "One thing I believe—that utterance is place enough," Emerson wrote to Carlyle in an 1834 letter that barely conceals his desperation at being in a state of ebb.[10] Of course "place" in that avowal has less to do with space than with status, as "utterance" has less to do with heard speaking than with externalization of thinking.

Speaking is a synecdoche for Emerson. The shaping of utterable words is part of a whole that is not so much unutterable as still-to-be-uttered. In "The Poet" the synecdoche is made clearer: "I know not how it is that we need an interpreter, but the great majority of men seem to be minors, who have not yet come into possession of their own, or mutes, who cannot report the conversation they have had with nature" (W, III, 5). In this seminal version of what Wallace Stevens will call Major Man, Emerson distinguishes the poet for his ability to report conversation, that is to speak speech. It is not in conversing with nature that the poet is unique, but in reporting that conversation. This relationship to speech should be seen as both a remove and an intensification; for just as leasts are both microcosms and minute but vastly consequential differences, so the remove of the reporting poet can also be an intensification. As a speaker about speaking, the poet is doing his work of appropriating the NOT-ME. That appropriation is necessitated by the recognition of separateness, and it is executed by the achievement of identity.

This achievement of identity is not, however, the mystical dissolution of self into all. An easy pantheism, a facile transcendence, and a heady selflessness characterize that sort of achievement. However keenly and reverently Emerson appreciates the beauties of such mergings, he is unequivocally devoted to another sort of discipline: not dissolution of self into all, but meta-

10. Slater (ed.), *Correspondence*, 109. Porte, *Representative Man*, 293–96, has a parallel discussion of the importance Emerson gives to speech and eloquence.

morphosis of all into self. The first Emerson saw as Oriental, the second Occidental. "If the East loved infinity, the West delighted in boundaries" (W, IV, 52).[11] The Oriental way of achieving identity through immersion, Emerson saw as a return to departed half-gods in the sort of regression that Owen Barfield has called idolatry.[12] Instead of such flight to immediacy the exercise of mediacy is indicated—the exertion of saying. Such saying is reporting; but it is both record and act because *what* it reports is conversation. What it reports is a relationship, a use of a disparity.

In reporting the conversation that all persons have with nature, the poet speaks a soliloquy that is a synecdoche for a dialogue. Call that soliloquy a part for a whole, by reason of its having one speaker where once there were two conversants; or call it whole for part, by reason of its combining into a unity what was once a dialogue. Either way the poet's speech is not about nature or about any other thing. It is a speech about speech. With its property of double substitutions, synecdoche is a figure that may be expected to appeal to Emerson because transforming parts into wholes is characteristic of Emerson's poetic program, and granting the grotesque partiality of any wholeness a mortal can pretend to is equally characteristic of Emerson's thinking.

Seeing Emerson's idea of speech as a synecdoche enables one to bring under critical scrutiny his habit of creating speakers through whom he himself speaks. From *Nature*'s Orphic poet to the less readily identifiable speakers in "Experience," the cast of characters is large and various. There is the solitary fellow traveler whose reported speech about the temptations and rewards of solitude forms the opening of the title essay of *Society and Solitude* (W, VII). There is Benedict, blessed speaker of "Worship," whom Emerson purports to "recall" as a "remarkable per-

11. See also W, X, 176ff.
12. See Owen Barfield's study of the history of consciousness, *Saving the Appearances: A Study in Idolatry* (London, 1959). The book owes much to such works by Rudolf Steiner as his cosmology, *Occult Science: An Outline* (London, 1963), a debt Barfield would be the first to acknowledge. Indeed, see Barfield, *Saving the Appearances*, 141, for a general acknowledgment of Steiner's work.

son whose life *and discourse* betrayed many inspirations of this [the moral] sentiment" (W, VI, 234; my emphasis). Such speakers bear the burden of Emerson's essays. Indeed, the following passage, from "Art," implies that their presence as actors in one of Emerson's arguments may testify to the burdensomeness of that argument.

> Thought is the seed of action; but action is as much its second form as thought is its first. It rises in thought, to the end that it may be *uttered and acted*. The more profound the thought the more burdensome. Always in proportion to the depth of the sense does it knock importunately at the gates of the soul, *to be spoken, to be done*. Speech is a great pleasure, and action a great pleasure; they cannot be foreborne. (W, VII, 38; my emphasis)

Whether or not these creations of Emerson's are indices of the profundity of his argument, they function as stand-ins who rehearse and extend the argument so unobtrusively as to seem either invisible or gratuitous. But these understudies for Emerson and these corroborators of his argument are as necessary to the drama of his interior oratory as the Chorus is to the progress of a Greek tragedy.

Usually they are too overtly externalized to be personae. Emerson often purports, after all, to have met these speakers on his travels and to be quoting them. And yet they are frequently too transparently Emersonian to qualify as novelistic characters, though they often are "characters" in the Theophrastian sense of exemplary portraits of psychological types. However they may be classified, Emerson creates and abandons these *ad hoc* seconders with such negligent self-reliance that it is easy to overlook their presence completely. I have sought, nevertheless, to catch some of these speakers in the act, hoping not only to explore a neglected feature of Emerson's rhetoric, but also to open the way to a better understanding of the informal tone and abrupt argumentation of his later essays. Even granting the primacy that utterance has for Emerson, it seems remarkable that his fables should so frequently be stories about situations in which something was said; and this is true whether the fables are spurious anecdotes about gods in their heavens or spurious reports of personages in Concord. Often an Emersonian fable of reported conversation will be a framed aphorism, an aphorism offered at one remove by being attributed to another speaker. In "Character," for instance, Emerson has just defined character as "a reserved force, which acts directly by presence and without means" (W, III, 89). Then, after some lines of explanation-by-restatement, he summarizes with, "His [*i.e.*, the man of character's] victories are by demonstration of superiority, and not by crossing of bayonets. He conquers because his arrival alters the state of affairs." Then, without further transition, without introduction, and without more warning than the presence of quotation marks, Emerson begins an original fable *in medias res* by reporting the following conversation:

> "O Iole! how did you know Hercules was a god?" "Because," answered Iole, "I was content the moment my eyes fell on him. When I beheld Theseus, I desired that I might see him offer battle, or at least guide his horses in the chariot-race; but Hercules did not wait for a contest; he conquered whether he stood, or walked, or sat, or whatever thing he did." (W, III, 90)

As far as I know Edward Emerson's note to the effect that this fable is original with Emerson is correct. Apparently Emerson's faith in fable is such that even a specious reference to mythology may be used to validate and vitalize an insight. At that, as Edward Emerson reveals in another note, "he pruned [such material] with a classic severity for his essays, [so that] many were omitted" (W, IV, 360–61). Those he did leave in, it may be conjectured, represent a necessary minimum of such informal but useful material. Since Emerson's own aphoristic articulation of his insight about character is so complete (notably, it comes at the start, the firmament-establishing section of the essay), it remains curious that he would indulge in the sort of extenuating emphasis his fable provides. But apparently the concept seemed elusive to Emerson and in need of such dramatic plasticizing. In any case, that fable is the story of a conversation and is, there-fore, a rhetorical variant of an aphorism—indeed, a vehicle (perhaps an excuse) for an extra aphorism.

If Iole's diction is suspiciously Emersonian for an Olympian, so is the diction of the traveler who, without warning or identification save the briefest of pedigrees, enters "Worship" to validate a point that is dear to Emerson—that "religion must always be a crab fruit; it cannot be grafted and keep its wild beauty." Instead of expanding discursively upon the Orphic insight—already, be it noted, couched in Yankee, or at least exoteric, terms—Emerson continues with the following reported quotation: "'I have seen,' said a traveller who had known the extremes of society, 'I have seen human nature in all its forms; it is everywhere the same, but the wilder it is, the more virtuous'" (W, VI, 214). And that traveler, like Iole, is no more conveniently Emersonian in diction and sentiment than is the unidentified but wholly identifiable "ironmaster" Emerson quite suddenly reports upon in "Considerations by the Way." Here, Emerson has been discussing the servant problem and has just murmured that "few people discern that it rests with the master or the mistress what service comes from the man or the maid; that this identical hussy was a tutelar spirit in one house and a haridan in the other" (W, VI, 275–76). It is a version of use, Emerson's theme in *The Conduct of Life* where "Considerations by the Way" constitutes a chapter. After some two sentences in which use by master or mistress starts to be conceived specifically as the generosity with which master or mistress sees fit to pay the servant, and without any warning that he is moving from declamation to reportage, Emerson continues, "When I asked an ironmaster about the slag and cinder in railroad iron,—'O,' he said, 'there's always good iron to be had: if there's cinder in the iron it is because there was cinder in the pay'" (W, VI, 276).

As instantaneously and unceremoniously as he is created, the ironmaster is abandoned—once he has performed his function, which is to plasticize and anthropomorphize Emerson's own aloof self, and to do so by speaking. Possibly, the "man of wit" in the following abrupt little anecdote is historical rather than fictitious, but one suspects that, like the speaker dubbed merely "a lady," who, Emerson reports, "complained to me that of her two maidens one was absent-minded and the other was absent-bodied," he is an *ad hoc* invention: "A man of wit was asked, on the train, what was his errand in the city. He replied, 'I have been sent to procure an angel to do cooking'" (W, VI, 275).

THEMSELVES CONDENSATIONS, Emerson's fables make the density of Emerson's condensed prose permeable when they explicate what is implicit in it. But so deep is the suggestive habit with Emerson that they also implicate while they explain, so that a double movement is effected. In his essay "Transcendentalist Catalogue Rhetoric: Vision Versus Form," Lawrence Buell identifies this double movement with cataloguing and with "what seems to be Emerson's purpose—to overwhelm us with the multiplicity of instances but at the same time impress us with the design inherent in these."[13] Illustrative detail functions suggestively in Emerson's prose as in any good fiction or poetry. Actually, Emerson's illustrative details are suggestive in two ways. One complicates; the other explains. Even the solely explanatory kind has an enlivening force that its implicitness tends to belie.

An example from "Resources," an essay that is in many other ways unsatisfactory, demonstrates the specifying and enlivening functions I refer to. In it the anthropomorphization both reduces and rarefies the more abstract statement, which is fairly summarized in these sentences: "The world belongs to the energetic man. His will gives him new eyes. He sees expedients and means where we saw none" (W, VIII, 144). This dictum articulates the theme of the collection of anecdotes that composes the essay. The essay's variety of instances helps insure that readers will understand correctly how Emerson means for the world to become their resource. Readers are to understand that the world does not become a resource by exploitation but by continuation, which is a form of appropriation. It is to secure this understand-

13. Lawrence I. Buell, "Transcendentalist Catalogue Rhetoric: Vision Versus Form," *American Literature*, 40 (1968), 332.

ing that Emerson adds, "The hunter, the soldier, rolls himself in his blanket, and the falling snow, which he did not have to bring in his knapsack, is his eiderdown, in which he keeps warm till the morning" (W, VIII, 144).

Emerson's excursions into exemplification can tire, and the profusion of anecdote in this particular essay (from the 1860s) is undoubtedly a poor substitute for the more rigorous drama of his best essays. Still, these homely exemplifications serve not only to clarify Emerson's idea, but also to characterize the appropriative powers of Emerson's mind. One feels, upon reading of the snowy eiderdown, that Emerson's mind must have been vigorously at its habitual work of placing and relating in order so suddenly, as it seems, to have produced the telling example. Such a fablelike illustration demonstrates that the enormous power of statement Burroughs attributes to Emerson involves a subtle capacity for variation that makes Emerson a master of repetition in Wallace Stevens' sense. "Perhaps," muses Stevens in *Notes Toward a Supreme Fiction*, "the man-hero is not the exceptional monster, / But he that of repetition is most master."

Though duplication and fragmentation were uncongenial to Emerson's love of newness and wholeness, he achieved a tolerance for repetition as well as skill at it. His humble and devoted acceptance of repetition is part of his charm. It is the earmark of his good cheer, and it is the manifestation of his sense of his office. That office was never mastery but always companionship; and it is Emerson's strength to have fulfilled it, sphinxlike, with riddling and fabulizing and exemplifying while nevertheless remaining paradoxically aloof and enduringly dignified. He is more accessible than approachable; he speaks and writes to be understood, not to be befriended, applauded, or—most distasteful of all—adulated. His leasts foster that precarious relationship with his audience. They invite complicity because they function suggestively not didactically. I do not seek your approbation of results, Emerson seems to say, I seek your partnership in experimentation. I disclaim persuasion; I offer demonstration in order to activate you, not convince you. The appeal is from one mind to another mind, not from one concept to a mind, or vice versa.

If Emerson's transcendentalism means anything at all, it means this peculiar bridge-building *over* rather than *between* the ostensible termini he is discussing.[14]

Consider Emerson's masterful passage on why Shakespeare is to be judged both for his "dramatic merit" and as a "poet philosopher." The mastery of the passage may be attributed to the way it elaborates by restatement, moving surefootedly from abstraction to concretion and from concrete generalization to universalized particularization. Throughout, the single idea that Shakespeare is too valuable as a thinker to be valued merely for his achievement as an artist—which achievement Emerson concedes to be matchless—remains the concept Emerson is arguing, and it is well served by each of Emerson's elaborations upon it. But the interest of the passage lies in the way Emerson's various particularizations surprise, and in the way the surprises enlist assent by seeming both to show his mind at work and to attribute to readers' minds a similar way of working. The first part of the quoted passage establishes that Shakespeare is to be valued for the quality of his insights not of his art; the second part seems to me to exemplify Emerson's engaging restatement.

Had he been less, we should have had to consider how well he filled his place, how good a dramatist he was,—and he is the best in the world. But it turns out that what he has to say is of that weight as to withdraw some attention from the vehicle;

. . . .

he drew the man, and described the day, and what is done in it; he read the hearts of men and women, their probity, and their second thought and wiles; the wiles of innocence, and the transitions by which virtues slide into their contraries: *he could divide the mother's part from the father's part in the face of the child*, or draw the fine demarcations of freedom and of fate: he knew the laws of repression which make the police of

14. Compare Kenneth Burke on the "seventh office" that persons perform for each other, that of "pontificating," bridge-building; in "I, Eye, Ay—Emerson's Early Essay 'Nature': Thoughts on the Machinery of Transcendentalism," in Myron Simons and Thornton H. Parsons (eds.), *Transcendentalism and Its Legacy* (Ann Arbor, 1966), 5.

nature: and all the sweets and terrors of human lot lay in his mind *as truly but as softly as the landscape lies on the eye.* And the importance of this wisdom of life sinks the form, as of Drama or Epic, out of notice. 'T is like making a question concerning the paper on which a king's message is written. (W, IV, 210–11; my emphasis)

From "he drew the man, and described the day" to the final simile with its appealing originality (and its barb at textual criticism of all kinds), Emerson's terms suggest his own ideal and his own mind at work more than they characterize Shakespeare's practice. Far from being a weakness, this is Emerson's purpose here as in all the meditative portraits that compose *Representative Men.* The sublimely apt yet utterly homely ratio whereby landscape is to sight as the psyche's terrain is to genius' insight works this way, for it makes us re-evaluate the ordinary fact that landscape surrounds us. The simile not only compares the achievements of genius to something we experience every day, but also reminds us that we do not realize we experience it every day. Thus Emerson is not just using the known to make the unknown accessible. In the same stroke by which he does that he also manages to "make the visible a little hard / To see" as Wallace Stevens was later to write that the worthy poet must do ("The Creations of Sound").

Using illustrative elaboration either to make the known special or to make the unknown accessible is of course common. Emerson's achievement is doing both at once. Emerson's simile offers a subtle insight that is neither about ordinary things like landscape nor about geniuses, but about an extraordinary relationship to all that is obvious and evident: Genius takes as given what others take for granted. When Emerson characterizes Shakespeare's keen moral discernment in terms of an ability to separate in the face of the child the mother's part from the father's part, his choice of those particulars for elucidation is equally arresting. Just as the landscape simile suggests reflection—even meditation—upon the obviousness of the obvious, so this startling attribution also works suggestively. It suggests Emerson himself ruminating on the phenomenon of a child's being able to resemble both of his perhaps extremely dissimilar parents. It suggests, too, that by the mother's or father's "part" Emerson does not mean just a mere feature as genetically duplicated in the child's face, but rather the subtler traces of parts each has played in begetting, bringing forth, and nurturing the child. Most of all, it suggests that Emerson's audience's habits of mind include, as do his own, such musing observation.

Emerson's technique assumes that something so common as the way children resemble parents is in fact a mystery worthy to test even the rare wisdom of the poet-philosopher. By assuming this, Emerson effects the kind of transformation his landscape simile treats of, because by assuming this he turns something taken for granted into a given. By making that transformation he turns his argument into his audience's chance to experience in the very way that his passage says geniuses experience. In short, like Emerson's Plato Emerson himself "keeps the two vases, one of aether and one of pigment, at his side, and invariably uses both" (W, IV, 66).[15] Emerson invariably uses both, and most often in such a way that the contracting pigment has the expanding effect of ether.

EMERSON'S COMIC touches and vignettes are an important form of his more personal style. Vivian C. Hopkins treats his humor in her study of his aesthetics, citing an excellent article by Henry Demarest Lloyd upon which most of her own remarks are based.[16] In common with other contemporary and near-contemporary appreciations of Emerson, Lloyd's article sees Emerson's humor as part of his seriousness, his eye for the ridiculous as part of his vision of the sublime, and his wit as part of his wisdom. It is astonishing and regrettable that Lloyd's article has not been reprinted in one of the collections of Emerson criticism, for it is not only shrewd, sane, and appreciative about the

15. Quoted by Tony Tanner, *The Reign of Wonder: Naivety and Reality in American Literature* (London, 1965), 44; see also Tanner's entire discussion, pp. 36–45.

16. Vivian C. Hopkins, *The Spires of Form: A Study of Emerson's Aesthetic Theory* (Cambridge, Mass., 1951), 194–97. Henry Demarest Lloyd, "Emerson's Wit and Humor," *Forum*, 22 (November, 1896), 346–57.

place of Emerson's humor in his thinking, but it preserves, as Hopkins notes, the oral tradition of jokes about Emerson. These apocrypha reveal a nice blend of veneration and ridicule for the Sage of Concord. Their humor contains a mixture of admiration and suspicion toward his detachment, and of pride and mistrust in his genius. While Lloyd offers a sympathetically chosen collection of Emerson's witticisms from the light to the profound, he is at pains to deny that there is craftsmanship in Emerson's humor. Apparently Lloyd fears that he may seem to be accusing Emerson of craftiness if he praises him for craftsmanship; thus Lloyd insists that "to round a sentence or play the oracle was not possible to his integrity and sanity." [17] I feel no such hesitation about crediting Emerson with designing his prose carefully and knowingly. The journals were unavailble to Lloyd. With their help it is possible to see not only how carefully Emerson pruned fables out of his essays but how carefully he pruned those he included. "Wealth" offers a case in point which will at the same time permit us to place Emerson's wit within the tradition of American humor. We shall see that offhandedness is a rhetorical gesture that argues not self-effacement (as Lloyd asserts) but self-reliance. For purposes of comparison it will be best to quote both the journal passage and the one from "Wealth," rather than attempting to proceed directly to summarizing and analyzing differences.

As the first two sentences of the journal passage make clear, the vignette is intended to dramatize the importance of knowing one's own direction and refusing to go in any other, no matter how alluring or how officially salutary. But first the finished passage as printed in "Wealth," then the journal study for it:

> With brow bent, with firm intent, the pale scholar leaves his desk to draw a freer breath and get a juster statement of his thought, in the garden-walk. He stoops to pull up a purslain or a dock that is choking the young corn, and finds there are

17. Lloyd, "Emerson's Wit and Humor," 357. Incidentally, by saying this, Lloyd ignores the significance of one of the apocryphal stories he records: the legend that when Emerson visited Egypt the Sphinx said to him, "You're another."

two; close behind the last is a third; he reaches out his hand to a fourth, behind that are four thousand and one. He is heated and untuned, and by and by wakes up from his idiot dream of chickweed and red-root, to remember his morning thought, and to find that with his adamantine purposes he has been duped by a dandelion. (W, VI, 115)

It seems often as if rejection [,] sturdy rejection [,] were for us; choose well your part, stand fast by your task, and let all else go to ruin if it will. Then instantly the malicious world changes itself into one wide snare or temptation,—escape it who can. With brow bent, with firm intent, I ⟨walk⟩ ↑ go ↓ musing in the garden walk. I stoop to pull up a bidens that is choking the corn, and ⟨ne⟩ find there are two; close behind is a third, & I reach out my arm to a fourth; behind that, there are four thousand & one. I am heated & untuned, and by & by wake up from my idiot dream of chickweed & ⟨bidens⟩ ↑ redroot ↓, to find ↑ that ↓ I with my adamantine purposes, am a chickweed & pipergrass myself. (JMN, X, 80) [18]

As I have indicated, the journal version makes the point of the vignette clearer than the essay version does. Presumably this is so because in the essay, context provides what the first two sentences give in the journal. The largest change effected in the essay is the substitution of third person for first. This substitution has the formalizing effect Emerson would be expected to seek. In addition, the distance the paragraph thereby achieves promotes a sense of caricature that is absent from the journal version. Even without knowing about Emerson's dislike for gardening chores and his ineptitude at them, one feels that "he" is "I" and that the caricature is self-caricature.[19] Consequently, the change from I, Emerson, to he, the "pale scholar," represents considerable gain at no loss.

Most of the other, smaller changes also increase the comic effect. They do so by heightening the drama to the point of the

18. I have preserved the JMN editors' marks indicating additions or insertions (↑ ↓) and cancellations (⟨ ⟩).

19. See W, VI, 116, n. 1 on Emerson and gardening.

mock-heroic. Whereas in the journal version a bidens is choking the corn, in the essay the corn is young and has two potential enemies, purslain and dock. The altered punctuation and redistribution of the word *and* in the subsequent clauses make them more staccato and thus at once more dramatic and more ridiculous in the essay version. The change in the morning revelation from "waking to find that I . . . am a chickweed & pipergrass myself" to waking to find that one "has been duped by a dandelion" is a similar change. The increased formality of the alliteration combines with the mock-heroic proportions of the realization to insure comedy. While the journal passage stops here, the essay continues through two more steps before it subsides from caricature into regular prose. In the first stage Emerson capitalizes on his improvements; to summarize the grotesque situation he has been rendering he creates a cartoon that anticipates Walt Disney: "A garden is like those pernicious machineries we read of every month in the newspapers, which catch a man's coat-skirt or his hand and draw in his arm, his leg and his whole body to irresistible destruction." The next four sentences modulate from cartooning to discoursing and from joke to earnest. First, a recapitulative exaggeration: "In an evil hour he pulled down his wall and added a field to his homestead." Then two aphorisms, the second extending the first: "No land is bad, but land is worse. If a man own land, the land owns him." And lastly, a final brandishing of the mock-heroic: "Now let him leave home if he dare." The level of the prose has been restored, and Emerson continues upon his theme, still in strong terms— "this pottering in a few square yards of garden is dispiriting and drivelling"—but now with an earned peevishness that remains controlled and becomes even-tempered precisely because controlled excess has preceded it.

Three more brief samples of Emerson's comic vein: There is the charmingly damning little fable about "Credulous Cockayne," the gentleman farmer who exemplifies the second rule of wealth, "Spend after your genius, *and by system*" (W, VI, 116; Emerson's emphasis). Credulous Cockayne, whose name would almost be worthy of Stevens, exemplifies the rule by breaking it, by being one thing—a businessman—and expending as another—a sometime farmer (W, VI, 120). If Credulous Cockayne's name is almost worthy of Stevens, so is Emerson's robust play with sound in the following outburst against mindless use of technology, where the onomatopoeic possibilities of the words *caoutchouc* and *guttapercha* are exploited as though they were Emerson's coinages: "What of this dapper caoutchouc and guttapercha, which makes water-pipes and stomachpumps, belting . . . and diving bells, and rainproof coats . . . which teach us to defy the wet, and put every man on a footing with the beaver and the crocodile?" (W, VII, 160). Lastly, for sheer economy of satiric invention, here is Emerson describing a platform bore. One can watch the speaker get less and less eloquent as he gets more mindful of his personal self and less mindful of his audience:

> Our country conventions often exhibit a small-pot-soon-hot style of eloquence. We are too much reminded of a medical experiment where a series of patients are taking nitrous-oxide gas. Each patient in turn exhibits similar symptoms—redness in the face, volubility, violent gesticulation, delirious attitudes, occasional stamping, an alarming loss of perception of the passage of time, a selfish enjoyment of his sensations, and loss of perception of the sufferings of the audience. (W, VII, 62)[20]

To watch the platform bore lose eloquence as his self-consciousness increases is to watch a comic version of Emerson's highly serious and deeply held conviction that bad speaking is bad manners. Emerson's comedy is a kind of controlled spontaneity that focuses comprehension and releases assent much as do Emerson's larger rhetorical practices and larger rhetorical formats. In addition there is the pleasure of surprise—surprise at the extent of Emerson's spleen on an innocent subject like going out to the garden to rest the mind, and at the thematic richness his simple spleen is made to produce. Emerson knew well that *altus* means

20. For a further sample of Emerson's invention and satire see the long paragraph in "Behavior," in which Emerson peoples a salon and satirizes it through the eyes of an expediently produced "high-born Turk," (W, VI, 184–85).

both high and deep, and everything about his synthesizing habit of mind enabled him to thrive upon the paradox.

Among other things, this paradox meant that overstatement and understatement are equally hyperboles. In his study of Emerson's prose style, André Celières pejoratively calls Emerson's hyperbole exaggeration, but he usefully cites the following instances.[21]

> I think nothing is of any value in books excepting the transcendental and extraordinary. (W, III, 32)

> History has been mean; our nations have been mobs; we have never seen a man. (W, III, 113)

> The people fancy they hate poetry, and they are all poets and mystics. (W, III, 16–17)

It seems to me that each of these supposedly damaging examples from Celières' collection is as much a self-reliant wildness as it is a self-indulgent excess. Each, moreover, exaggerates in order to state, rather than in order to persuade. This last is even truer of the following slightly longer sample, in which the very subject is proportion and exaggeration: "Art, in the artist, is proportion, or a habitual respect to the whole of an eye loving beauty in details. And the wonder and charm of it is the sanity in insanity which it denotes. Proportion is almost impossible to human beings. There is no one who does not exaggerate" (W, III, 234). The near-exaggeration of the penultimate sentence modulates brilliantly into the final sentence, which may be either true or an exaggeration but not both. From this witty contriving of Emerson's it seems clear that he is discoursing hyperbolically on exaggeration by design not by default.

In a helpful note to Emerson's lecture on "The Superlative," as printed in *Lectures and Biographical Sketches*, Edward Emerson quotes from one of Emerson's notebooks:

> The excellence of what I call the *Low Superlative* is shown in

---

21. André Celières, "The Prose Style of Emerson: Thèse Complémentaire pour le Doctorat D'Etat presenté à la Faculté d L'Université De Paris" (Paris, 1936), 25.

Newton's praise of Cotes, "If he had lived, we should have known something." Or in the *mot* which I found in D'Herbelot, "If the poems of Dhoair Fariabi fall into thy hands, steal them, though it were in the temple of Mecca;" or in Tom Appleton's speech about Shakspeare [*sic*], "He'll do."

"The whistling of cannon-balls affected him so unpleasantly that he withdrew" from the army. (W, X, 168, n. 1)

Notably, Emerson includes both over- and understatement in his list of low superlatives. Indeed, it is in their understatement that each (except for the *mot* of D'Herbelot) is hyperbolic, as Emerson's term for them denotes. Each is a miniature tall story.

Such delight in the tall story as a version of the high figure is a Yankee trait. In her classic study, *American Humor*, Constance Rourke summarizes the amalgam between low and high, practical and idealistic, homely and revelatory, circumstantial and exemplary that one finds in Emerson as in his countrymen. Rourke's immediate reference is to the humor of Sinclair Lewis, but her summary serves us here because it recapitulates much that earlier parts of her study had developed in connection with America's earlier humor and humorists. First, Rourke attributes to Lewis' humor "that highly circumstantial fable-making which has been a characteristic American gift." (By "circumstantial" is meant "rooted-in-circumstance.") She then continues to cite the tradition:

> The material is prosaic, the mood at bottom romantic; gusto infuses the whole, with an air of discovery. Even the derision is not a new note. . . . [It] is part of the enduring native self-consciousness; it is seen here, as before, in a close tie with the comic. Lewis uses homely metaphors that might have been spoken by Yankee Hill. . . . The familiar biting understatement appears, and the inflation.[22]

The prosaic material, the fundamentally Romantic mood, the gusto, the air of discovery, the comic derision, and the biting understatement—all these are features of Emerson's leasts. In addi-

22. Constance Rourke, *American Humor: A Study of the National Character* (Garden City, N.Y., 1955), 223.

tion, Emerson's leasts are "low key" and "subtle in . . . range,"
like the Yankee strain Rourke finds in American humor, while at
the same time exhibiting—perhaps even more typically—the
qualities Rourke distinguishes in backwoods humor: "Backwoods drawing was broad, with a distinct bias toward the grotesque, or the macabre." As Rourke goes on to point out, the
Yankee and backwoodsman strands intertwine to make one
American humor; and the important thing about that American
humor is that it is thoroughly fantastic despite its often crude
materials. "The fantasies . . . might be crude and earthy, but they
were fantasies. These odd and variegated creatures were firmly
planted in the spacious realm of legend." [23]

The spacious realm of legend suited the humor of dwellers in
the spacious New World, because it could include the intensities
of myth and the popularization of folktale, the polished fable
and the spun yarn, and because it could mix the virtues of each
eclectically and democratically. As a learned rather than a rustic
humorist, Emerson had a particularly large repertoire of myth to
mix with more personal matter. From it he could draw for his
own, original legends the characters whose allegedly legendary
doings and conversations he could adduce to empower his argument. The homemade legend cited earlier, about how Iole recognized Hercules to be a god, is one example. Another is the fable
with which Emerson ends "Manners."

It is a tall story that masquerades as a high figure, though ge-
nially, not deceptively, so. In an Olympian setting, Olympian
personages talk of godly prerogatives—whether or not to destroy the earth—in New England vocabulary; and they settle the
question by means of a Yankee standard. According to Edward
Emerson, the fable is original despite the phrase about "a tradition of the pagan mythology" with which Emerson introduces
it as a gloss upon the question of whether or not society and
its fashion are worthy of preservation and adherence. (The
form of the fable, it will be noted, is again that of a reported
conversation.)

Too good for banning and too bad for blessing, it [*i.e.*, society] reminds us of a tradition of the pagan mythology. "I overheard Jove, one day," said Silenus, "talking of destroying the earth; he said it had failed; they were all rogues and vixens, who went from bad to worse, as fast as the days succeeded each other. Minerva said she hoped not; they were only ridiculous, little creatures, with this odd circumstance, that they had a blur, or indeterminate aspect, seen far or seen near; if you called them bad, they would appear so; and there was no one person or action among them which would not puzzle her owl, much more all Olympus, to know whether it was fundamentally bad or good." (W, III, 155)

The entire essay ends with this Yankee retort of Minerva's, as quoted by Silenus, venerable satyr and companion to Dionysus, and recorded by Emerson. For Emerson to settle, or rather, rest, the vexing question of society's worth in this ostentatiously disengaged way is for him to imply that if he himself were to settle it, it would have to be done another way.

The abruptness of the ending constitutes the implication. Such abruptness, whether at ends or middles, is vintage Emerson. It is Emerson taking his own advice to orators: "If you desire to arrest attention, to surprise, do not give me facts in the order of cause & effect, but drop one or two links in the chain, & give me with a cause, an effect two or three times removed" (JMN, VII, 90). Here, the dropped or missing ending of "Manners" suggests that the answer to society's worth rests not upon the worth of the society but upon the worth of its members. "Of what use to make heroic vows of amendment, if the same old law-breaker is to keep them?" asks "Experience" (W, III, 51), and with that rhetorical question answers the one that puzzles Minerva's owl. Of course it is not always true that a dropped link suggests the link from another chain that would supply the gap. But it is always true that Emerson's abruptness is suggestive and that the paratactic placement of his fables or vignettes or aphorisms functions—like the juxtapositions of catalog rhetoric—to specify by absence. "The poet knows the missing link by the joy it gives" (W, VIII, 10), and recognition of Emerson's own missing links offers that poetic joy to his readers.

THIS MATTER of suggestive absence brings us back to the question of leasts as minute differences with huge consequences. "There is a crack in every thing God has made," Emerson declares in "Compensation" (W, II, 107). That statement is not a complaint but a confirmation. It confirms the most difficult and fundamental principle Emerson holds—the principle that there is such a thing as the uncreated. If the glory of that principle is the conviction that the uncreated exists as Over-Soul (or as Emerson more usually calls it, Power) within every created thing, the accompanying, verifying sorrow of that conviction is this: Everything is either Maker, and thus whole but unrealized, or Made, and thus realized but cracked. Thought itself is not immune to the imperfection: "The intellect that sees the interval partakes of it, and the fact of intellectual perception severs once for all the man from the things with which he converses" (W, XII, 44). Moreover,

> It is not to be concealed that the gods have guarded this privilege [of being able to think] with costly penalty. This slight discontinuity which perception effects between the mind and the object paralyzes the will. If you cut or break in two a block or stone and press the two parts closely together, you can indeed bring the articles very near, but never again so near that they shall attract each other so that you can take up the block as one. That indescribably small interval is as good as a thousand miles, and has forever severed the practical unity. (W, XII, 44)

Between these two dire acknowledgments that the discerning power of thought is power to make only because it is power to crack, the lecture version had a fable that was excised from the printed version. The fable makes an even more dire statement about the subversively effective power of the mind to destroy unity. Aemilius is stabbed by Velent's sword, which is so sharp "that its entrance into the body could hardly be perceived," according to the fable. " 'I feel thy sword,' cried Aemilius, 'like cold water, gliding through my body.' 'Shake thyself,' said Velent. He did so, and fell down dead in two pieces."[24] It is not known whether Emerson or his editor omitted this fable from the "Powers and Laws of Thought" section of *Natural History of Intellect*. If Emerson did the cutting, it may have been because the fable distorts an important corollary of the subversiveness of thought which it dramatizes so clearly. The corollary is that unity and identity are not the same thing. When unity eventuates in identity, the cost is as dire as what had happened to Aemilius; but the cost is birth, not death. The fate of Aemilius obscures this principle.

It is, however, the principle that differentiates boundaries from limitations. "The only sin is limitation," says "Circles" (W, II, 308), because limitation is finality. Identity, however, is, in "Circles" as everywhere in Emerson, not limitation but possibility. Every identity is, anew, a manifestation and therefore a source of power. Identity is severance from unity. In being bounded by additional surfaces, each new identity becomes, indeed proliferates, that infinite repellency that, far from diminishing power, continues immortally its externization.

Emerson was fascinated by boundaries both in their capacity as definitive leasts and for their identification of vital differences. "*La nature aime les croisements*," he several times quotes from Fourier.[25] Cross-breeding, whether in his pear orchard or his imagination, represented to him supremacy *over* limitation *by means of* limitation. Whether by hiatus or demarcation, the presence of a boundary confirms for Emerson the presence of a new identity, and thus the presence of Power. "Napoleon stands at the confluence of the two streams of thought & of matter, and derives thence his power" (JMN, IX, 178). Similarly, from the essay "Power":

In history the great moment is when the savage is first ceasing to be a savage, with all his hairy pelasgic strength directed on

24. Quoted by Edward Emerson, W, XII, 44, n. 1.
25. See JMN, IX, 50 and 365; W, VII, 162; W, VIII, 289; W, XII, 25–26.

his opening sense of beauty:—and you have Pericles and Phidias, not yet passed over into the Corinthian civility. Everything good in nature and the world is in that moment of transition, when the swarthy juices still flow plentifully from nature, but their astringency or acridity is got out by ethics and humanity. (W, VI, 70–71)

The ultimate confirmation is the confirmation of the primal principle—the confirmation of power; and the cost of that confirmation is submission to proliferation. Why does submitting to proliferation confirm the advent of power? Precisely because the advent of power makes cracks, because the advent of power makes identity not unity. The attitude of mind that sees this way is not a perverse optimism but an optimum perversity. That is the attitude Emerson cultivates with his leasts no less than with the more substantial elements of his style. For Emerson, the nature of power is that it must externalize itself and do so ruinously; but each of its ruins will also constitute one of those infinitely repellent particles by means of which, as "Experience" puts it, (W, III, 68), "the mind goes antagonizing on."

IV
The Risks of Affirmation: "Compensation" and "Self-Reliance"

> But the soul that ascends to worship the great God is
> plain and true, has no rose-color, no fine friends, no
> chivalry, no adventures; does not want admiration;
> dwells in the hour that now is, in the earnest experience
> of the common day,—by reason of the present moment
> and the mere trifle having become porous to thought
> and bibulous of the sea of light. (W, II, 290)
>
> Demonology is the shadow of Theology. (W, X, 28)
>
> You would compliment a coxcomb doing a good act,
> but you would not praise an angel. The silence that ac-
> cepts merit as the most natural thing in the world, is
> the highest applause. (W, I, 148)

 ust as the confirming Emerson is to be found most readily in *The Conduct of Life* and "Experience," so the affirming Emerson is most typically revealed in *Nature* and *Essays, First Series*. Still, the principle that cost is confirmation for Emerson is as true of *Nature* and *Essays, First Series*, as it is of the later work. To approach the earlier works with this principle in mind is to find that they are more complex, more flexible, and also more durable than their affirmative mode suggests. Accordingly, it will be useful now to focus on these two books and on Emerson's consciousness of the burden their affirmations impose on him and on fellow adherents whom he may find or create among his audience.

Emerson knows that there is nothing lucky or comfortable about belief. Belief does not give relief; it incurs obedience. Conviction does not release one from uncertainty, but rather bonds one to service. In this sober, even dire spirit, Emerson offers his ringing charge to "Trust thyself: every heart vibrates to that iron string" (W, II, 47); or his fervent affirmation of compensation whereby "our act arranges itself by irresistible magnetism in a line with the poles of the world" (W, II, 110); or his exploration, in *Nature*, of "the harmonies that are in the soul and in matter, and specially of the correspondence between these and those."[1]

Correspondence, compensation and self-reliance are the iron wires on which all of Emerson's work is strung. They are so braided that they are hard to distinguish, yet each is a principle with a characteristic province. Compensation and self-reliance are cosmic principles, and correspondence is a principle of language.

OF THE three, compensation was perhaps the dearest to Emerson. "Ever since I was a boy I have wished to write a discourse on Compensation," he opens his essay so entitled.[2] Among his reasons for this wish was his conviction, first, "that on this subject life was ahead of theology and the people knew more than the preachers taught." Theology and its spokesmen are disqualified by life and those who live it from experiencing this principle, but, since resigning the Second Church pastorate in September, 1832, Emerson himself has been an antitheologian and, despite regular invitations to preach, a former preacher. As such he is now free to try to fulfill his boyhood aspiration, though he is quick to acknowledge its awesomeness: "happy beyond my expectation if I shall truly draw the smallest arc of this circle" (W, II, 96).

Second, "the documents too from which the doctrine is to be drawn, charmed my fancy by their endless variety" and by their proliferation everywhere—in "the transaction of the street, the farm and the dwelling-house; [in] greetings, relations, debts and credits." They "lay always before me, even in sleep" (W, II, 93), their obsessive presence being at once an assurance of their importance and of their concordance with Emerson's vocation as

1. Ralph L. Rusk (ed.), *The Letters of Ralph Waldo Emerson* (6 vols.; New York, 1939), I, 435.
2. See also Slater (ed.), *Correspondence*, 120–21.

pulpitless, parishless orator. Moreover, an eloquent discourse on the subject of compensation offered two further possibilities to that orator—the chance to affirm the value of "the present action of the soul of this world clean from all vestige of tradition" and the lure of so articulating that affirmation that the statement "would be a star in my dark hours and crooked passages." It would be an external and public guide as reliable as the "bright *in*tuitions" by means of which the doctrine "is sometimes revealed" privately (W, II, 93–94).[3]

The opening of this integrally important essay, then, announces that it is the climax of thirty or more years of wishing and dreaming.[4] Curiously, however, Emerson's argument itself is about the perniciousness of desire. Wherein, after all, lay the insidious fallacy contained in the sermon on the Last Judgment which, Emerson goes on to say, he has recently heard "unfolded in the ordinary manner," by a preacher "esteemed for his orthodoxy" (W, II, 94)? "The fallacy lay in the immense concession that the bad are successful; that justice is not done now" (W, II, 95). Justice *is* done, and it is done *now*. That is the constant affirmation of "Compensation." Its equally constant but subtler admonishment is that to believe otherwise is to make an immense, unworthy concession. It is to concede to "the base tone of popular religious works of the day," to the "doctrine assumed by the literary men," to the specious decorum and actual superstition of "our popular theology." In short, compensation involves self-reliance, not reliance on some externally proposed doctrine ("men are better than their theology"). Consequently, the insidious reliance on some future when "we are to have *such* a good time as the sinners have now" (W, II, 95; Emerson's emphasis) is to be shunned.

Emerson scorns reliance upon some future restitution of a supposed deprivation as being the dangerous consolation of or-

3. Although Emerson does not italicize the prefix of "intuition" he is clearly tapping the word's etymological energy. Compare the "Divinity School" address on the moral sentiment: "[I]t is an intuition. It cannot be received at second hand" (W, I, 126–27).

4. On the composition of "Compensation," see W, II, 396–97.

thodoxy. He is equally stern about the very sense of deprivation itself. For instance, in the following passage from "Spiritual Laws," which Emerson regarded as a chapter that completed his discourse on compensation, Emerson declares that repining a loss is itself a weak and weakening response: "If in the hours of clear reason we should speak the severest truth, we should say that we had never made a sacrifice. In these hours the mind seems so great that nothing can be taken from us that seems much. All loss, all pain, is particular; the universe remains to the heart unhurt" (W, II, 131).

By placing *unhurt* after *heart* instead of before it Emerson can qualify both the perceiving heart and the abiding universe with the one adjective. As a result this final sentence means that to the unpained heart the universe remains intact and only to the heart that is in pain is it lost or impaired. When loss is experienced as pain, the hurting heart is the cause of discomfort, not the effect. Individual need puts one beyond the pale of compensation; only the self who believes in compensation so severely that it refuses to feel loss can have the benefit of compensation. (Compare this analogous austerity from "Worship": "If he is insulted he can be insulted" [W, VI, 233].) In order to have compensation when you need it, you have to manage not to need it.

Emerson was already deeply acquainted with personal loss when he was writing the material for *Essays, First Series*. His first wife had died in 1831, his brothers, Edward and Charles, in 1834 and 1836; and this is not even to mention the death of Emerson's father in 1811 when Emerson was not quite eight years old. He deeply revered loss as opportunity ("When half gods go, / The gods arrive") but deeply suspected it as temptation. The sense of loss, or of a current deprivation relative to another's apparent possessions, was suspect because it could disable the steadying perception of compensation, leaving the self-proclaimed loser not just apparently deprived but actually lost.

"There is somewhat low even in hope," Emerson warns a bit bemusedly, halfway through his most famously optimistic essay, "Self-Reliance" (W, II, 69). Like the belief in a last rather than a current judgment, hope is an unworthy attitude when it represents a gain "in decorum and not in principles over the superstition it has displaced" (W, II, 95). For truly to displace superstition is not just to offer the faithful a new decorum but to announce a new principle, and this transforming sort of announcement is the goal of Emersonian affirmation.

Emerson's awareness that superstition masquerades as decorum constitutes the motivation behind his attack on orthodoxy—in "Compensation" and in the rest of *Essays, First Series,* as well as in addresses and lectures of the 1830s. For all his belief in fable, his delight in lore, and his affinity for romance, Emerson has an abiding mistrust, even abhorrence, of superstition. "The word Miracle, as pronounced by Christian churches," he says in the "Divinity School" address, "gives a false impression; it is Monster. It is not one with the blowing clover and the falling rain" (W, I, 129). Unless the miracle correspond it is not reliable but monstrous. He consciously constructs his affirmations to bear the burden of maintaining this mistrust of miracles. That burden is the refusal to make concession to the merely marvelous, while at the same time justly wondering at the wondrously just and reliable universe. He *was* a long while finding his form, as Henry James knew; and, as James also knew, his message he had from the start.[5] Emerson's career, like his essays, begins with the sorts of climactic certainties that more orthodox quests end with. Yet Emerson is a quester nevertheless. Defining himself as a quester he says that he is "an endless seeker with no Past at my back" (W, I, 318), and he further characterizes himself with "a believer in Unity, a seer of Unity, I yet behold two" (JMN, V, 337). Accurate as these famous avowals may be to emphasize Emerson's characteristic insouciance about history and his repeated assaults upon the paradox of bipolar unity, they are misleading as characterizations of Emerson's search for a form. The essays aim to be tests of the strength, not of the truth, of his long-held message. They do not move from doubt to certainty, but from certainty to exemplification. This distinction is important because once his quest is seen as moving within a certainty

5. James, *Partial Portraits,* 6.

rather than toward it, the movements and moods of the quester become the gestures of a revealer not of a prover.

Describing himself in such a search, Emerson might better have described himself as a believer in miracle who yet saw monster. Whereas the usual function of instances is to establish certainty and persuade one of truth, Emersonian elaboration is different. For him the truth is not tested by the instance; the instance is salvaged or translated—or, to use his term, made transparent—by the truth. His is not a quest for the certainty required by a hypothesis, but for the vigor required by a certainty—the vigor to turn even monsters into confirmations of principle.

A brief further look at "Compensation" will illustrate how rich is the Emersonian accommodation between monster and miracle. The law of compensation both assures one that an abiding justice operates in the universe and commits one to being a willing exemplar as well as beneficiary of its workings. True, "there is no tax on the knowledge that compensation exists and that it is not desirable to dig up treasure" (W, II, 123). Yet the knowledge is taxing, if not taxed. Providing memorable illustration of a cost that confirms rather than depletes, "Compensation" ends with the image of a "sunny garden flower" that has been turned by apparent mischance and neglect into "the banian of the forest yielding shade and fruit to wide neighborhoods of men." The image not only provides a magnificently appropriate ending for the essay's affirmation that orthodox avidity is inept and unseemly, but reveals also a full consciousness of how seemingly exotic a growth unorthodoxy is. With roots that strike adventitiously into the soil to anchor its branches, a banian tree seems a monster compared to a garden flower. But the strength of image and essay, and the measure of the vigor of Emerson's argument, is precisely that *this* monster *is* miracle, is produced by the very wind and rain whose wild, benign force a walled garden and a prudent, pruning gardener would have worked wrongly to mitigate. It is not just that apparent calamity becomes actual power, but that the risks of seemingly irresponsible and damaging exposure yield a redeeming, if apparently bizarre, value.

Emerson struggles to construct his affirmations of a truth so as to house its most extravagant versions. He seeks to admit these as unorthodox collocation rather than as orthodox dislocation. Pairing his early lecture, "Demonology" (1839), with its final essay form (1877) makes a revealing study of this struggle with the risks of affirmation. Whereas the lecture's initiative ending is identical with the essay's, the two beginnings differ in tone, or gesture, though not in argument. Both beginnings announce the subject by name and define its components with the same list of six species belonging to the genre; both beginnings take sleep for the first topic to be investigated; and both investigations of sleep make the same points—that the fact of dreaming is a suprising renunciation of "deifying Reason" and that "there is one memory of waking and another of sleep" (W, X, 3 and 5; EL, III, 152 and 153). As they proceed, both the essay and the lecture use the same quotations and allusions, including the wonderful story of Masollam who summarily shot a bird of alleged omen in order to prove that "had he [the bird] known anything of futurity, he would not have come here to be killed by the arrow of Masollam the Jew" (W, X, 15; EL, III, 159–60). Both essay and lecture follow a long quotation from Goethe's *Dichtung und Wahrheit*, about the mysteriousness of the demoniacal, with identical preferences for daylight over "these twilights of thought" and with the confession that Emerson finds it "somewhat wilful . . . when men as wise as Goethe talk mysteriously of the demonological" (W, X, 10; EL, III, 166).

Throughout, then, both essay and lecture agree that even with so seemingly extravagant a phenomenon as the demonic, the indicated response is not the sensationalist one of proof but the worshipful one of use. As with the language of behavior, so with the language of extraordinary signs: its readability, not its existence, is what matters. Because of Emerson's early and abiding conviction that use not proof is the proper attitude toward truth, and that the way to meet truth is with power not with marveling, both lecture and essay share identical initiative endings. Despite all this unanimity, however, the lecture and the essay do not share identical climactic beginnings.

This fact is important because it demonstrates that Emerson

has an early ambivalence toward the uses of the marvelous, though he has no ambivalence about its existence. Compare the two openings. First, the 1877 essay: "The name Demonology covers dreams, omens, coincidences, luck, sortilege, magic and other experiences which shun rather than court inquiry, and deserve notice chiefly because every man has usually in a lifetime two or three hints in this kind which are specially impressive to him. They also shed light on our structure." But notice how much more tentatively—and with how much more hesitation before his topic's supposed unorthodoxy—Emerson began his lecture in 1839:

> There is a class of facts which though they seem rather to shun than to court the inquiry of the philosopher, have in every man's experience left some impression and at times and in some minds have disputed with reason and religion the direction of life. I refer to the topics of Dreams, Omens, Coincidences, Luck, Sortilege, Magic, and a large variety of facts which are supposed to indicate the presence of some foreign, unacknowledged element in nature that produces exceptions to, if not violation of, the ordinary laws. It is usual to rank these obscure facts under the general name of Demonology; and as each individual has usually in a lifetime two or three hints of this kind that are extraordinarily impressive to him, for this and for the light they throw on our constitution, they crave our consideration. (EL, III, 151–52)

The essay accomplishes in one long sentence what the lecture did in three. Moreover, the essay's short second sentence represents a certainty about the application and therefore the legitimacy of demonological phenomena—they "shed light on our structure." Whereas the essay thus announces from the start—somewhat awkwardly to be sure—the structural status of demonological phenomena, and announces it without question or apology, the lecture's opening does not cover the uses of demonology at all (unless one wished to count the glancing reference to "our constitution"). Instead, the lecture's attempt to deal with the uses, and therefore the legitimacy, of demonological phenomena does not come until the following passage from the last quarter of the lecture, a passage omitted entirely from the essay: "A large portion of the facts called demonological are not questions of theology or of metaphysics, but semi-medical questions, respecting our structure, very fit to be explored doubtless, and ranging themselves with the wonders of organization; but nowise entitled to be ranked in the category of the supernatural" (EL, III, 167).

The point is not that Emerson's essays are more compressed than his lectures, nor that in his seventies he was more convinced of this thesis than he was in his thirties. Rather, the point of contrasting lecture and essay is to show that the later work achieves a more suitable emphasis and arrangement for insights and convictions Emerson has held from the start. The comparison of lecture and essay reveals no change in his willingness to accept demonological phenomena, nor even any change in his conviction that it is indecorous superstition to emphasize them as extravagance from principle instead of as confirmation of principle. Although he knows that extravagance must be used to reveal rather than obscure lawfulness, he also knows that orthodoxy would rather relegate these matters to a convenient unorthodoxy than become itself so dangerously flexible as to include them. And in his thirties and forties Emerson is uneasy with that knowledge. This is why his announcement that the demonological is structural rather than deviant comes late and defensively in the lecture, but assertively and as part of the opening climax in the essay. As both lecture and essay declare in closing, "the whole world is an omen and a sign. Why look so wistfully in a corner?" (W, X, 28; EL, II, 170). The operative word is *wistfully*, as much as it is *corner*.

As might be expected, the essay "Heroism" is instructive for a study of Emerson's quest to integrate the exceptional so as to raise rather than to level. Stoicism does not quite cover the subtle blend of serenity and vigor that Emerson is characteristically advocating here. "Heroism" is preceded and complemented by "Prudence" in *Essays, First Series*, as in the important lecture series, Human Culture, read in the winter of 1837–1838, from which both were taken. While this pairing, like that of "Love" and "Friendship" in the same volume, suggests moderation and stoicism, "Heroism" itself is in search of a compendious virtue that is both simpler and rarer than the foregoing and forebearing fortitude that the word *stoicism* suggests. Emerson looks for a defiant affability: "that which takes my fancy most in the heroic class, is the good humor and hilarity they exhibit [in the face of calamity]" (W, II, 255). At the same time the moderation Emerson values is the extreme temperance of King David. In contrast to the abstemious Indian apostle, John Eliot, who drank water instead of wine, King David "poured out on the ground unto the Lord the water which three of his warriors had brought him to drink at the peril of their lives" (W, II, 254–55).

Heroism is to behavior in general as demonological phenomena are to signs in general; all are to be not so much reduced as expanded to the common, for the common is the truly miraculous.[6] Moreover, every miracle is suspect and dangerous until it can be perceived, or made, to be common. "The essence of greatness is the perception that virtue is enough. Poverty is its ornament. It does not need plenty, and can very well abide its loss" (W, II, 255).

If Emerson does not learn until "Experience" how to celebrate what he there calls "this poverty, however scandalous" (W, III, 81), he has already identified it here as the desirable, not just the desiring, state. Moreover, he explicitly identifies the desiring state with "the little man . . . [who] is born red and dies grey, arranging his toilet, attending on his own health, laying traps for sweet food and strong wine, setting his heart on a horse or a rifle, made happy with a little gossip or a little praise" (W, II, 252). Does this little man desire too much or too little? Both. He desires too little, too intently. It is, of course, a question of Emily Dickinson's "adequate desire." It is a question of adequate desire, not just any desire, as it is a question of scandalous poverty,

6. Tanner, *The Reign of Wonder*, 1–45, holds that, since Emerson, "naivety has become an important form of wisdom" in American literature (p. 35) and that "in encouraging men to 'wonder at the usual' Emerson bestowed perhaps his greatest benefit on American literature" (p. 45).

not just any poverty. Orthodox desire and poverty are not scandalous enough to be adequate. So the same Emerson who, I am holding, suspects desire for the way it reduces the quester to a weakening avidity is the Emerson who respects desire for the way it can expand the quester to a demanding openness. And one means "demanding" in both senses, of course.

In *Figures of Capable Imagination*, Harold Bloom calls this enterprise and capacity to expand "divination."[7] The wild spareness (or spare wildness) that advocates such divination, Bloom calls "Orphic asceticism." Discussing this peculiar sort of asceticism, Bloom has just quoted from "The Poet" the passage that ends, "That is not inspiration which we owe to narcotics, but some counterfeit excitement and fury" (W, III, 28). "This may sound merely conventional or even tiresomely sensible," Bloom comments, "but like Whitman's almost pathological emphases on purity and cleanliness and Dickinson's obsession with her White Election, it is a sublime passage of Orphic enthusiasm and about as ordinary as Whitman on death and the mother or Dickinson on what and how she merely sees." Having thus both named Emerson's paradoxical attitude toward striving, and placed that seemingly anti-Romantic sense of quest solidly within American Romantic tradition, Bloom goes on to say that this Orphic asceticism is a "peculiar kind of purgation," is "mostly the process of unlocking our gates, of opening ourselves to vision," and is "strangely American" in that this purification seems to be a matter of "release rather than repression."[8] Bloom's interest in the purgative quality of this Emersonian openness is peripheral to our present argument, but his identification of a rigorous, ascetic expansion is central to it. Precisely the requirements of this expansion are what Emerson is learning to include in his famous, early affirmations of its possibility, its efficacy, and its necessity.

The quest for openness can be achieved without travel, without killing or courting, and without marveling. In "The Poet,"

7. Harold Bloom, *Figures of Capable Imagination* (New York, 1976), 75.
8. *Ibid.*, 79.

for instance, Emerson describes how reading a poem "which I confide in as an inspiration" can be that quest and also its fulfillment. For the day of that reading can be "better than my birthday; then I became an animal; now I am invited into the science of the real" (W, III, 121). Possible as this rebirth through poetry may be, however, Emerson immediately points out that poetry's invitation is usually a seduction. What has been confided in as inspiration is usually a specious guide and stimulus: "Oftener it falls that this winged man, who will carry me into the heaven, whirls me into mists . . . still affirming that he is bound heavenward; and I, being myself a novice, am slow in perceiving that he . . . is merely bent that I should admire his skill to rise" (W, III, 12). Notice the terms of the deception: the quester has been invited to admire rather than to experience, to marvel rather than to ascend. Oftener than not, the promised fulfillment fails; the quest fails. What characterizes that failure? A petty exaggeration: "I tumble down again soon into my old *nooks*, and I lead the *life of exaggeration* as before" (W, III, 12–13; my emphasis). Exaggeration is the opposite of inspiration, or ascension, or expansion; it is not their means or their end.

And yet "the world is perennial miracle," as both the end of "The Over-Soul" and the end of the final lecture in Human Culture aver (W, II, 297; EL, III, 356). The miracle is omnipresent but only fitfully accessible. It is constant as cause, however inconstant as manifestation or effect. It is clear as thought, however murky as action. It is reliable as source, however demanding as goal. The confirming Emerson knows how to use this rarity of access to ratify preciousness; and the greatness of "Experience" is precisely that Emerson there finds a way to pay tribute to the rarity of apperception that makes miracle both common, in that it is omnipresent, and uncommon, in that it is so rarely accessible.

For Emerson to displace the value, function, and scope of two Romantic staples, wonder and desire, in the way I have tried to describe is for Emerson to redefine the nature of the quest which is traditionally generated by desire and sustained by wonder—the Romantic quest. The peculiarly Emersonian quest resulting from this displacement of wonder and desire is a surprising one. Instead of obviating questing altogether, Emerson's affirmative way of making wonder and desire a problem rather than a given results in a quest that moves from certainty to adequacy rather than from doubt to certainty. It becomes not a quest for knowledge one does not have but a quest for power to match the knowledge one cannot repudiate. The affirming Emerson is searching for the form, the conceptual gesture, that can make the announcement of grandeur a call to its concomitant demands, rather than assurances that are liable to become, too quickly, re-assurances—mere "complacencies of the peignoir," as Wallace Stevens will call them. Such a call is a call to quest within, rather than toward, certainty; and Emerson's constant problem is so to contrive the call that it can affirm certainty without denying the primacy of "the richest of all lords"—use (W, VI, 243). Nowhere is this problem more critical than in what is perhaps Emerson's most affirmative essay, "Self-Reliance," the articulation of his most dangerously popular principle.

"INSIST ON yourself, never imitate." "Trust thyself; every heart vibrates to that iron string." "Whoso would be a man, must be a nonconformist." This style of address is hazardous. Such ringing declaratives and imperatives can easily be detached as slogans. Used this way their meaning is distorted, of course. Their assertion of originality becomes license to deviation and even deviousness, while their call to individual power becomes an invitation to ignore the realities of communal life. Detached from its context, Emersonian self-reliance is popularly seen as precisely this sort of rugged individualism.[9] But self-reliance is not self-making. It is self-being or self-finding. Ultimately, it is God-reliance. In consequence, tracing American individualism—whether rugged or ruthless—to Emersonian self-reliance is as

---

9. A telling example is Gary Wills's 1969 study of Richard Nixon, *Nixon Agonistes: The Crisis of the Self-Made Man* (New York, 1971). Even in a serious and literate work like this one, Emerson and "Self-Reliance" are repeatedly cited as the source of the dangerous tradition in which, as the subtitle announces, Richard Nixon is seen to belong.

unsound as tracing Nazi sadism to Wagner's or Nietzsche's brands of the heroic. F. O. Matthiessen is careful to prevent such distorting reductions of the heroic in *The American Renaissance*:

> What saved Emerson from the extremes of rugged Emersonianism was the presence not merely of egoism but also of a universal breadth in his doctrine that all souls are equal. What stirred him most was not man's separateness from man, but his capacity to share directly in the divine superabundance.
> . . . .
> He wanted to study the laws of the mind, what he called throughout life the natural history of intellect, but he always felt a repugnance to self-centered introversion. . . . He held that there was "a pernicious ambiguity in the use of the term *subjective*." On the one hand, it could simply mean . . . a morbid self-indulgence. On the other hand, "a man may say I, and never refer to himself as an individual"—such is the valid subjectivity that arises from the perception that "there is One Mind." [10]

Matthiessen's astute quotation of Emerson on the use of the first person singular, and his useful phrase "valid subjectivity" may serve us to distinguish facile popularizations of Emersonian self-reliance from the richer and nobler doctrine that Emerson actually intended. [11] At the heart of this distinction lie two paradoxically related facts. The first is the nature of the self as Emerson sees it. The second is the deeply social function—even mission— of relying on that self as Emerson sees such reliance.

Who is this self? Where is this self found? And when? "The Over-Soul" answers the questions of when and where. When? In the moments of epiphany whose brevity is directly proportional

10. Matthiessen, *American Renaissance*, 8–9. See W, XII, 314, and EL, III, 215.

11. On individualism and the nineteenth-century progressive tradition see Daniel Aaron, "Emerson and the Progressive Tradition," in Konvitz and Whicher (eds.), *Emerson: A Collection of Critical Essays*, 85–99. Aaron quotes de Tocqueville's important distinction between selfishness and individualism and explicates "Emerson's ambivalent attitude toward aggressiveness and self-seeking," arguing that Emerson's "transcendentalism . . . provided an ideal explanation for the conduct . . . of the business classes and offered the necessary criteria by which he was able to justify or criticize them."

to their revelatory reality, says the essay's opening paragraph (W, II, 269). Where? From the prepositional adjective of the title, through the essay's final prepositional phrases, Emerson negligently mixes spatial words as he characterizes and locates the Over-Soul: It is "a light [which] shines through us" "from within or from behind" (W, II, 270); it is "Jove [who] nods to Jove from behind each of us" (W, II, 278); it is a "central commandment" (W, II, 281); and, in the essay's final words, it is "the negligency of the trust which carries God with it and so hath already the whole future in the bottom of the heart" (W, II, 297). In "Literary Ethics," Emerson speaks of "the superincumbent spirit" (W, I, 182); perhaps he should have adopted this term. In any case, whether it be over or inner, behind or central, or in the bottom of the heart, this soul is, like Saint Augustine's God, "a circle whose centre [is] everywhere and its circumference nowhere," as Emerson starts the next essay, "Circles," by declaring. The step from this God, omnipresent in space and time, to this God as the self to be relied upon is not a large one to make. Emerson makes it—and answers the question of Who?—in numerous ways and places; but two lectures—one early and one late—do it most explicitly. "Nothing but God is self-dependent," Emerson says in his introductory lecture to the 1836–37 series, The Philosophy of History (EL, II, 17). And in the second Fugitive Slave Law Address, the one he delivered in New York in 1854, he proclaims, "Self-reliance[,] the height and perfection of man [,] is reliance on God" (W, XI, 235).

The self which may be relied upon as guide on the quest that is a quest *within* certainty, not a quest *for* certainty, is God. Self-reliance is God-reliance. Moreover, that self who is God and is by definition self-dependent is not a psychological entity but a spiritual one. As spiritual entity, the self is a principle rather than an achievement or a technique; and relying upon it is obeying its commands, worshipping it as the Beautiful Necessity. Emerson has not yet learned to call self-reliance by this name, as he will in his ultimate essay on the subject, "Fate"; but already he is certain of its essence. In the rhapsodic ending of "Self-Reliance," he characterizes both the obedience it entails and the result it creates as "the triumph of principle":

In the Will work and acquire, and thou hast chained the wheel of Chance, and shall sit thereafter out of [that is, free of] fear from her rotations. A political victory, a rise of rents, the recovery of your sick or the return of your absent friend, or some other favorable event raises your spirits, and you think good days are preparing for you. Do not believe it. Nothing can bring you peace but yourself. Nothing can bring you peace but the triumph of principles. (W, II, 90)

Though no event, however favorable, can ever be a substitute for this "triumph of principles" that is "yourself," events themselves are decisively affected by the successful or unsuccessful operation of self-reliance. Or, to put it another way, as "Nothing but God is self-dependent" (EL, II, 17), everything but God is dependent. On God. Thus the second fact about self-reliance—its social importance—is entailed by the first fact about self-reliance, that the self is God. "For the sense of being which in calm hours arises, we know not how, in the soul, *is not diverse* from things, from space, from light, from time, from man, but one with them and proceeds obviously from the same source whence their life and being also proceed" (W, II, 64; my emphasis). No matter how individualistically and iconoclastically Emerson may choose to proclaim self-reliance, he never forgets that the distinction between valid and invalid subjectivity is always a question of forming a right relation to things, to persons, to the cosmos itself. Yet if that "sense of being" which is true God-reliance is not solipsism, neither is it gregariousness.

Whoever or whatever the participant in a self-reliant relation, it is always a relation that "is not made but allowed," as Emerson puts it in some sentences from "Character" that are worth quoting more fully: "It was a tradition of the ancient world that no metamorphosis could hide a god from a god. . . . Friends also follow the laws of necessity . . . their relation is not made but allowed" (W, III, 112). In short, self-reliant relations are elective affinities, and the mark of the reliable self is the capacity to elect, or remain open to, proper affinities by shunning specious ones. For, as "Spiritual Laws" puts it, "Nothing is more deeply punished than the neglect of the affinities by which alone society should be formed, and the insane levity of choosing associates by others' eyes" (W, II, 406).[12]

Notice Emerson's stern choice of the word *insane* when he makes this point. Here is a gloss on Emerson's choice, from "Society," the seventh lecture in the Philosophy of History series: "Among those who have lost their reason, among the insane[,] there can be no society" (EL, II, 99). Far from being a principle of anarchy, then, self-reliance is a principle of social order. Indeed, it is *the* principle of social order. For sovereignty and selfhood are metaphoric equivalents in Emerson's lexicon. In "Politics," for instance, another lecture from the Philosophy of History series, he declares that "reverence thyself" is the "voice of Reason" and that "its effect . . . goes to make [one] not a citizen but a state" (EL, II, 71). Here the metaphor marks the result of self-reliance as it also does in the "American Scholar" address where Emerson uses it to describe how "man shall treat with man as a sovereign state with a sovereign state" when, and only when, each individual is surrounded "with barriers of natural respect" (W, I, 113).

Just as sovereignty marks the triumph of principles which is self-reliance, so slavery marks the defeat of those same principles. When self-reliance is at issue, the stakes are extreme. Undoubtedly, this is why Emerson's rhetoric is so extreme in the essay that officially articulates the principle—"Self-Reliance." An example of the extreme rhetoric Emerson uses in "Self-Reliance" is the famous sentence about giving the "wicked dollar which by and by I shall have the manhood to withhold" from unsuitable suitors (W, II, 52). I want to examine closely the long and brilliantly written paragraph that ends with this famous reversal of philanthropic ideals and proprieties, because Emerson is here dramatizing the importance of self-reliance by considering instances that reveal it in the breach rather than in the observance. In other words, he dramatizes various misalliances that occur when the sovereignty that is self-reliance is abdicated.

12. Edward Emerson's amusing note to this passage records that "when somewhat importunately urged to be presented to a person for whom he felt no affinity, Mr. Emerson said, 'Whom God hath put asunder, let no man put together'" (W, II, 406).

The paragraph begins, "Whoso would be a man must be a nonconformist" (W, II, 50–52). As the passage proceeds it turns into a kind of mock masque that consists of a procession of seductive petitioners who beset Emerson (or whatever one should call the Protean speaker in this essay). The procession includes a philanthropist who sues for such "miscellaneous popular charities" as "the education at college of fools," "the building of meeting houses to . . . vain end[s]," "alms to sots," and all "the 1,000-fold Relief Societies." By way of answer to this hapless philanthropist and his multiple petition, Emerson speaks a single, monosyllabic question: "Are they *my* poor?"

The imperious rhetorical question is not, however, answer enough for another petitioner, the one whose character and claims Emerson's mock masque most fully develops. This character is the "angry bigot [who] assumes this bountiful cause of abolition, and comes to me with his last news from Barbadoes." For the purpose of hypothetically dismissing this suitor, Emerson has his allegorized, reliant self deliver a speech that turns out to be brilliant self-parody. To read it, with its commands and declarations and iconoclasm, and its insouciant egotism, is to experience the risks and vitality of "Self-Reliance" in miniature and in caricature: "Why should I not say to him, 'Go love thy infant; love thy wood-chopper; be good-natured and modest; have that grace; and never varnish your hard, uncharitable ambition with this incredible tenderness for black folk a thousand miles off. Thy love afar is spite at home.'" [13]

Even including the satiric parodies of physicians and phrenologists in "Experience," there is no more daring and self-knowing passage of hyperbolic fabulation in all of Emerson than this decimation of the bigot abolitionist. Although Emerson favored secession if abolition could not be managed, his journals leave no doubt that he strongly supported abolition, however irritated he might sometimes feel by various of its spokesmen. For Emerson to reject even a hypothetical petitioner in this contro-

13. For the journal version of this passage, see JMN, V, 370. For related journal passages see JMN, V, 437 and 505.

versial and incendiary cause represents a real risk, clearly calculated to be an index of self-reliance's importance in the hierarchy of causes. But of course it is not a question of causes, and this is the main message conveyed by the rhetorical risk Emerson has taken. It is a question of relations—those "relations not made but allowed," which are Emerson's elusive theme in this essay.

"Thy love afar [it is easy and productive to misread "affair" here] is spite at home." Emily Dickinson defined God as home, and Emerson would have concurred.[14] The relation to home, to God, is self-reliance; and to show how drastic an effort it is to allow such relation, Emerson not only risks but invites incredulous response to his Nietzschean transcendence of conventional moral standards. This technique of hyperbolic nay-saying is designed to confirm what must be the final, as it is the initial, yes-saying.

Although in his masque passage Emerson loftily refuses to stop and "spend the day in explanation," he is clearly aware throughout "Self-Reliance" that "it is the fault of our rhetoric that we cannot strongly state our fact without seeming to belie some other," as he has already deplored in the volume's opening essay, "History" (W, II, 39). Actually, Emerson is in masterful control of his poses and ventriloquisms; and he consents, later in "Self-Reliance," to step down from the platform of parody and speak as friend and aider of all those who seek a self-reliant conduct of their lives.

In order to affirm that self-reliance is infinity manifested as conduct, he has had to speak as that devil's child whom he had said he would willingly admit to being if maintaining self-reliance required it (W, II, 50). Now he changes his rhetorical strategy (though not his vigorous, challenging tone) and confronts directly the misunderstanding that he knows his pronouncements of self-reliance attract. "The populace think that your rejection of popular standards is a rejection of all standards, and mere antinomianism" (W, II, 74). (Notice how much

14. Richard B. Sewall, *The Life of Emily Dickinson* (2 vols.; New York, 1974), I, 270.

ierson gets from the word *mere* and from his etymologi-
/ming of *popular* with *populace*.) To deal with this misun-
anding Emerson goes on to distinguish "two confessionals,
ne or the other of which we must be shriven." You may clear
yourself "in the *direct* or in the *reflex* way," he elaborates. The
reflex way looks to others to see "whether any of these can up-
braid you" for not discharging the duties of your relations to
them. In contrast, the direct way is to "absolve me to myself."
Far from being an evasion of either accountability or relations
with others, the direct way of absolution requires measurement
against "one's own stern claims and perfect circle" (W, II, 74;
Emerson's emphasis). Moreover, one cannot just elect this
sterner way of accounting; one may "dispense with the popular
code" only when one is able to perform the sterner kind of accounting. Thus, the direct way imposes a double commandment:
One must not only prefer it to the reflex way; one must qualify
for that preference.

Emerson ends this passage with the warning, "If any one
imagines that this law is lax, let him keep its commandment one
day" (W, II, 74). The dire and yet humble directness of that pronouncement makes it a culmination of all the slogans, examples,
hypothetical fabulations, and stern exhortations that have preceded. At the same time the passage makes a bridge to the remaining third of the essay, which illustrates the revolutionary
potential of self-reliance by ranging among instances of the
ruinous consequences that attend lapses of self-reliance. The
bridging paragraph combines the godlike character of self-
reliance with its societal purpose and mission: "And truly it demands something godlike in him who has cast off the common
motives of humanity and has ventured to trust himself for a task-
master. High be his heart, faithful his will, clear his sight, that he
may in good earnest be doctrine, society, law, to himself, that a
simple purpose may be to him as strong as iron necessity is to
others!" (W, II, 75).

Two important, revealing phrases figure in this combination
of the visionary and the political that introduces the last third of
Emerson's great if repetitious affirmation of self-reliance. The

first is "as iron necessity." It is a telling phrase because it reminds us that at this point in his career Emerson sees only self-reliance's similarity to the iron necessity of others and of circumstances, not yet its identity with the Beautiful Necessity of one's self and of fate.[15] It also serves to remind us that the important part of conduct for Emerson is motivation, despite his shrewd preference for action over intention. Motivation is the problem that affirming self-reliance raises for Emerson. As such, it bears the same relationship to self-reliance that wonder and desire do to compensation. That is, just as affirming compensation entails reassessing wonder and desire, so affirming self-reliance entails reassessing motivation. Emerson is conscious that his affirmations of self-reliance impose the requirement to reassess motivation. This consciousness is a burden that acts as a ballast. It weights the buoyancy of his message while at the same time steadying his argument, directing his search for a form.

In reassessing motivation, Emerson seeks to reconcile his spiritual conviction that motive is the mystery of conduct with his psychological observation that intention is far from insuring achievement or giving it worth. As usual, "Experience" is the essay that will manage this delicate alignment of observed fact with causative principle: "The sentiment from which it sprung determines the dignity of any deed, and the question ever is, not what you have done or forborne [notice that doing and forbearing have equal status as conduct], but at whose command you have done or forborne it" (W, III, 72). Here Emerson achieves reconciliation by looking to a deed for its dignity not its success. Once this transvaluation is achieved, evaluating conduct remains possible. Emerson does not have to retreat into some noncommittal pluralism or some exotic solipsism. Instead, he can measure the dignity of deeds by a standard that is neither absolute nor relativistic, because it is not a standard of adherence in the ordinary sense. It is a standard of obedience to requirements that

15. At that, see "History," W, II, 5: "Every reform was once a private opinion and when it shall be a private opinion again it will solve the problem of the age." Used also in the introductory lecture to the Philosophy of History series, EL, II, 15, where it reads somewhat differently.

have been discerned, not imposed; and such requirements do not *make* relations, they *allow* them. Such requirements upon the doer of a deed therefore become—or can become—elective affinities. As elective affinities they do not affect deeds unless the doer chooses that they should.

Just as "adequate desire" generated by sufficiently "scandalous poverty" animates the Emersonian quest, so these "relations not made but allowed" motivate and validate the Emersonian deed. Clearly, the question "at whose command" a deed is "done or forborne" is a question that must be asked continuously by every self-reliant conductor of life. Clearly, too, the power to ask that question is the power that self-reliance both demands and generates. If self-reliance is a true possibility, asking that hard question is what it costs. Affirmations of self-reliance will not be honest unless they recognize this entailment, and they will not be effective unless they grant its claims. In "Self-Reliance" Emerson meets the formal challenge of his message through hyperbole and parody (including self-parody that is both biographical and stylistic). Brilliant as these strategies are, they make the essay somewhat shrill and self-conscious. Functioning more as tactic than as form they indicate self-reliance's hazards, but do not fully confirm self-reliance's power. In a later work, however, Emerson does succeed in incorporating the issue of motivation, whereas in "Self-Reliance" he had to create scenes that only pointed to its problematic importance. The work I refer to is the Fugitive Slave Law Address of 1854. This is the text that best clarifies the confirming costs that Emerson's doctrine of self-reliance entails.

AT THE start of this discussion of self-reliance, the second of Emerson's three fundamental doctrines, I indicated that Emerson explicitly defined it as God-reliance. Moreover, he did so not in "Self-Reliance," not in the "Over-Soul," not in "Circles," not in any of the essays of *Essays, First Series,* nor in the addresses and lectures of the 1830s, but precisely in the 1854 Fugitive Slave Law Address. It may seem curious that Emerson's most topical, engaged discourse should contain the most explicit statement of self-reliance's divine status; but close examination of this powerfully crafted and unjustly neglected address reveals that it is "Self-Reliance" written as an occasional piece.[16]

The occasion, of course, is the fourth anniversary of Daniel Webster's famous speech favoring the passage of the Fugitive Slave bill, part of the Great Compromise bill of 1850. Three years earlier Emerson had addressed his Massachusetts neighbors on this treacherous desertion of the cause of liberty by this influential statesman, but the issue still demands Emerson's attention.[17] He gives it reluctantly, but unstintingly, in a new address crafted for this more distant audience and tempered to a finer hardness by four years of reflection on America's struggles to save the Union. The entire speech has rhetorical as well as substantive affinities with the essay "Self-Reliance." It displays before its audience the age's most spectacular and damaging misalliance of a self, Webster, with the age's most damaging and ignoble institution, slavery. It also proceeds according to a program of decimation that is as dramatic—even suspenseful—as the masque-like passage in "Self-Reliance," with one important difference; here allegory has become history and hypothetical petitioning has become politics.

The decimation has two targets. After a climactically significant and beautiful opening to which I shall return below, Emerson offers such a detailed memoir and characterization of Daniel Webster that Webster seems to be the address's subject and the target of its stern, measured, and sustained anger. For some seven paragraphs Emerson recalls for his audience how "Mr. Webster, by his personal influence, brought the Fugitive Slave Law on the country." He remembers for his audience the "natural ascendancy of aspect and carriage which distinguished

16. K. Laurence Stapleton, *The Elected Circle: Studies in the Art of Prose* (Princeton, 1973), 176, says that the Fugitive Slave Law Address "should be included in every selection of [Emerson's] work." See Stapleton's entire commentary, 176–80.

17. For the earlier address see W, XI, 177–214. For an informative discussion of Emerson's increasing involvement with the issue of slavery during the 1850s, see Gonnaud, *Individu et Société*, 457–67. See also JMN, XI, 279–365, and xv–xvii.

[Webster] over all his contemporaries," and remembers how, at Bunker Hill, Webster "stated his fact pure of all personality, so that his splendid wrath—was the wrath of the fact and the cause he stood for" (W, XI, 219, 221, 222).

If Webster's wrath was splendid then, Emerson's is now. For all his eminence, natural leadership, and even eloquence (by which word Emerson, recall, habitually means divinity), Webster is finally charged with lacking the one critical faculty without which all his talents and achievements are not only worthless but harmful. "If his moral sensibility had been proportioned to the force of his understanding, what limits could have been set to his genius and beneficent power: But he wanted that deep source of inspiration" (W, XI, 223). Lacking that deep source, Webster's words lacked what Emerson most valued as the mark and result of true eloquence—lustres: "There is not a general remark, not an observation on life and manners, not an aphorism that can pass into literature from his writings" (W, XI, 224). From another speaker such a complaint might be querulous and anti-climactic. From Emerson it is, of course, definitive. It is equally characteristic that Emerson first points to this critical deficiency of Webster's and only then asks the thundering question to which the fact of this deficiency is already the answer: "Nobody doubts that Daniel Webster could make a good speech. Nobody doubts that there were good and plausible things to be said on the part of the South. But this is not a question of ingenuity, not a question of syllogisms, but of sides. *How came he there?*" (W, XI, 225; Emerson's emphasis).

As one of Emerson's auditors, James C. Gibbons of the New York *Tribune*, wrote to his son two days after hearing the address, "Emerson gave us a fine lecture on Webster. He made him stand before us in the proportions of a giant; and then with one word crushed him to a powder." [18] Gibbons' response to the address does justice to Emerson's dramatic eloquence, but it is not a summary of Emerson's full achievement nor of his deepest purpose in this address. For Gibbons' summary neglects the fact that Webster is only one of Emerson's targets, and the minor one

18. Quoted by Edward Emerson, W, XI, 589–90.

at that. Part of the strategy of Emerson's address has been to disguise from his audience that he has a second and major target, and that they themselves are it. At this point in the address, however, it becomes clear that the state of these voters, not the state of Daniel Webster, is Emerson's target and his topic. The question "How came he there?" marks the close of the attack on the statesman and the opening of this more serious attack on his followers. Indeed, on following at all.

This occasional version of "Self-Reliance" is not so much about the self as it is about reliance. Circumstances have driven Emerson to making reliance, not the self, the issue. And once the connection between the address and "Self-Reliance" is made, it becomes clear how extensively the essay, too, concerns the demands of reliance and the risks of misalliance, and how these demands and risks are the entailments of what both essay and address are affirming.

As Emerson redirects his address toward its true target, he follows the same strategy he had used for his attack upon Webster. He does not merely berate his audience; he credits the existence of their motivations, acknowledges how understandable these are, and then pronounces them incontrovertibly wrong. As always he is both shrewd and magnanimous in his understanding of motivation. Acknowledging the natural tendency toward conservatism that he as a man of property shares with his audience of voters, he finds conservatism a quite appropriate response to ownership. But he concedes that fear motivates such conservatism, and obedience to the commands of fear is a motivation he cannot condone.

Fear is the antithesis of liberty and "the world exists . . . to teach the science of liberty, which begins with liberty from fear" (W, XI, 232). His audience has failed to learn this "first lesson" precisely to the extent that it has relied on a covenant out of fear instead of relying each on himself or herself as a "minority of one" (W, XI, 235).

> You relied on the Constitution. It has not the word *slave* in it. . . . You relied on the Supreme Court. The law was right excellent law for the lambs. But what if unhappily the judges

were chosen from the wolves, and give to all the law a wolfish interpretation? You relied on the Missouri Compromise. That is ridden over. You relied on State sovereignty in the Free States to protect their citizens. . . . And now you relied on these dismal guaranties infamously made in 1850; and, before the body of Webster is yet crumbled, it is found that they have crumbled. (W, XI, 233)

With its repeated condemnation, "You relied," this passage establishes the Fugitive Slave Law Address as the occasional version of "Self-Reliance" that it has been developing into from its beginning. It has been a speech that began by stressing the self only to reveal that the real issue is not self but reliance, that the real crime is not *being* Webster but *following* Webster. "No man can come near me but through my act," warned "Self-Reliance" (W, II, 72). The Fugitive Slave Law Address anatomizes the act by which we allow an attachment that should have been kept detachment. Fear and the wishful reliance on supposed guarantees are the operatives in such an act. Those "dismal guaranties" that have crumbled as fast as Webster's own body "are not guaranty to the free states. They are a guaranty to the slave states that, as they have hitherto met with no repulse they shall meet with none" (W, XI, 234). Earlier in his speech Emerson had shrewdly analyzed the Fugitive Slave Bill as an index of the slave states' strength and the free states' weakness by saying that "it discloses . . . that Slavery was no longer mendicant but was become aggressive and dangerous" (W, XI, 229). Later, Emerson reinforces the point that fear is the force behind the passage of the bill by recalling Montesquieu's caustic observation, "It will not do to say that negroes are men, lest it should turn out that whites are not" (W, XI, 238). Such self-protection can never be the way of self-reliance, because self-protection precludes the openness whose vulnerability is the risk that confirms the value of self-reliance.

Emerson's scorn and anger have two edges in the 1854 address. One is his outrage at the impediment to sovereignty that the Fugitive Slave Law constitutes. Sovereignty, as we have seen, is a metaphor for the reliant self. Its opposite is not society, therefore, but mob. As "Self-Reliance" puts it in a passage that wonderfully democratizes its own arrogance, "The world has been instructed by its kings" (W, II, 63). Instructed to follow kings? No, to emulate the way kings have "magnetized the eyes of nations," to emulate the way a king commands "joyful loyalty . . . by a law of his own" (W, II, 63). In short, self-reliance is a principle of the Emersonian democracy whose point is not that every king is really just a man like you and me, but rather that each of us is really a king.

The second edge to Emerson's scorn and anger in the Fugitive Slave Law Address is his outrage that this bill makes it impossible for him to be both civilly and morally obedient. Because moral obedience is always in service to liberty whereas this law serves not liberty but fear, the law has made a fugitive and thus a slave of Emerson. As slavery becomes tyrannical ruler, sovereign selves become slaves who are coerced by a law that fear has made them pass against their own sovereignty and "on the miserable cry of Union" (W, X, 229). Quite consciously Emerson lets his very lexicon implicate him and his audience in the outrage at hand, so that the address becomes even more than the double attack it is so skillfully constructed to be. It becomes a transcendentally candid confession of shared guilt, even as it remains a passionately challenging exhortation to distinguish the speeches of disabling fear from the dictates of ameliorating liberty and to cooperate with these latter by refusing to capitulate to the former.

Indeed, the address's last word is *cooperation*. Its last rhetorical gesture is a peroration aiming to instill faith in the amelioration that "will not save us but through our own cooperation" (W, XI, 244). Individual and free as self-reliant deeds must be, free doers are bound in a community of believers—of votaries— whose votes must cooperate with amelioration if they are not to impede its profligately slow but inexorably victorious operations.

According to the reading I have been developing, the Fugitive Slave Law Address confirms self-reliance's power by incorporating the burdens imposed by self-reliance's truth. These burdens are ultimately the burdens of cooperation, burdens that are peculiarly difficult for Emerson to assume. Assuming them seems to Emerson to violate both his own faith in self-reliance and his own mastery of the standards of free obedience it entails. Emerson's own reluctant assumption of these alien burdens is precisely the topic he chooses for the opening of his address. Notice how Emerson's deep reluctance to speak tempers his climactically beautiful and powerful opening sentences to so deft and candid a simplicity that his words both reveal and transcend his consciousness of the ironies of the situation: "I do not often speak to public questions;—they are odious and hurtful, and it seems like meddling or leaving your work. I have my own spirits in prison;—spirits in deeper prisons, whom no man visits if I do not" (W, XI, 217).[19] The believer in unity is having to show his audience that preserving moral union with the cause of freedom may entail the disruption of an existing political and economic union. The believer in private, solitary, and reflective action is called to a public arena to discuss a public action. Emerson starts with this self-reliant report about his own conflict concerning self-reliance. With this report he turns on himself the question, "How came he there?"—the question he will ask about Webster and will challenge his audience to ask about itself.

What is strong enough to make Emerson abandon his patient, self-reliant visits to his own imprisoned spirits—strong enough, indeed, to make him allude publicly to their existence even as he abandons his cherished duty to them? What is strong enough to draw Emerson into this "dissipated philanthropy" that is "odious and hurtful" because of the "havoc it makes with any good mind?" The claims strong enough to exact such tribute from Emerson are not the claims of a principle, or a doctrine, or an institution. They are the claims of an affinity, Emerson's affinity with "the well-being of students and scholars everywhere."

> It is only when the public event affects them that it very seriously touches me. And what I have to say is to them. For every

19. For "spirits in prison," see 1 Peter 3:19. In an 1834 journal reflection upon a visit to the zoo, which is instructive to compare with the present passage, Emerson uses the same Biblical text (JMN, IV, 296–97, and n. 135).

man speaks mainly to a class whom he works with and more or less fully represents. It is to these I am beforehand related and engaged, in this audience or out of it—to them and not to others. And yet . . . the class of scholars or students . . . is a class which comprises in some sort all mankind, comprises every man in the best hours of his life. (W, XI, 217–18)

With an honesty that transforms reluctance by matching it, the orator of the interior here acknowledges that he is "beforehand related and engaged" and announces that in making this address he is keeping that engagement and fulfilling that relation. It is an engagement with an audience, a relation to their well-being.

Loftily Emerson proceeds to define that audience as a class that "comprises . . . every man in the best hours of his life." As he does so, he performs—even in this minor key—his act of creating the ears that are to hear by speaking to them as if they could already hear. This concentration upon audiencehood, the sober evocation by invocation, and the quiet transformation of exhortation into commitment—these features mark how the Fugitive Slave Law Address differs from the essay "Self-Reliance." And this difference measures the full potential of self-reliance, as essay and as message in search of a form.

Where the essay focuses on conviction and on acting from conviction, the address presents itself as an act against conviction. Where the essay stresses that every man is a king (not that every king is really just a man like any other), the address must deal with the fact that if any man is a slave every man is a slave. While the essay opens by contrasting the too-ready regard we give to another's thoughts with the too-hesitant regard we accord our own, the address opens with a confession that Emerson has had to abandon his own solitary thoughts in order to shake loose the too-dependent thinking of his audience. To be sure, the address's opening moment and its opening emotion are brief and quiet compared to the dramatic attacks, and shrewd analysis, and passionate challenge that succeed it. But the opening is definitive, even so.

It defines the occasion as an odious demand that Emerson nevertheless fulfills willingly. It implicates both Emerson and his audience in the occasion and thereby binds that audience into a community that can cooperate in revolt against its own guilt. The question to be thundered about Webster—"*How came he there?*"—is already implicit in Emerson's own presence here, and each auditor has to ask it about himself. Further, discovering the answer to this question must always involve deciding "at whose command" one is doing or forbearing. Most importantly, the address's candid and affecting introduction defines what is at stake when self-reliance is at stake: the functioning of sanity in service of those "relations not made but allowed" that constitute true society. "Nothing," it will be remembered from the start of our discussion of self-reliance and society, is more deeply punished than the neglect of these relations by substituting for them the "insane levity of choosing associates by others' eyes." [20] Not that Emerson is here confessing to any such insane levity in appearing before this audience. He is confessing to having had to overcome the suspicion that his appearance here might be such an insane and ultimately antisocial choice. He is further confessing what he would have been doing had he stayed home. He would have been visiting his "own spirits in prison;—spirits in deeper prisons whom no man visits if I do not." With that image Emerson does three things.

First, he speaks in philanthropic terms about staying home. Second, his philanthropic terms suggest that the people before him are themselves prisoners whom he now visits instead of those others and that they are spirits in shallower prisons whom too many have visited while Emerson did not. Third, for Emerson to present the speech he is about to make as a visit from a free man to prisoners is for Emerson to imply his audience's unseen jailer. That jailer is fear. And so is the jail. Since the fear belongs to these prisoners, their imprisonment is self-imposed and their release may be self-achieved. If this audience is its own jailer, it is also, potentially, its own liberator. It must minister unto itself in this situation, for to visit oneself in prison is precisely to refuse to be jailer and jailed, and instead to elect to be

20. See pages 110–11, herein.

visitor and visited. To be visited by oneself is to be visited by the Over-Soul within, by God. Such a visitation is the liberation Emerson is here to bring about by proposing it. We have seen the attacks and challenges by which he proceeds to do this, and we have seen that these attacks and challenges describe the power for alliance and misalliance that resides with Emerson's auditors to use or fail to use. We have not yet focused sufficiently on the deep punishment that would attend misuse of the power to free and be free. Emerson does deal with that punishment and, in doing so, most fully indicates the results of abandoning self-reliance.

SINCE THE opposite of self-reliance is what Emerson in the Fugitive Slave Law Address calls "the habit of oppression," the results of exercising or permitting this habit are the results that define these stakes and this punishment. What are the results of oppression? "The habit of oppression cuts out the moral eyes, and, though the intellect goes on simulating the moral law as before, its sanity is gradually destroyed. It takes away the presentiments" (W, XI, 237). The habit of oppression, which is the abdication of self-reliance, "takes away the presentiments." It "cuts out the moral eyes." Thus nothing less than "the moral eyes" are at stake when self-reliance is at stake. For these presentiments, these moral eyes, are the faculty by which one perceives one's relations to the Over-Soul within. Without such perception there can be no God-reliance, no self-reliance; just as *with* such perception the triumph of principles that is self-reliance will already be occurring.

If this triumph and condition are what Emerson has risked in coming to New York to address his audience, they are also what his audience has risked in needing Emerson's ministrations. The fact that Emerson risks these stakes because he discerns this audience's need as a compelling claim upon him does not diminish the risk. Rather, the risk measures the value of the renunciation and at the same time shows that the audience's need is its prison. Only if they can stop needing self-reliance and start exercising it, instead of exercising the habit of oppression, can they have the benefits of self-reliance. What was true of compensation in its way is true of self-reliance in its way; in order to have it, you have to manage not to need it.

Self-reliance is not an asocial principle, but a profoundly social one. It is also a capacity, a faculty. Indeed, Emerson repeatedly presents it as a faculty in "Self-Reliance." He presents it as a faculty that enhances its own potential when it is exercised and that atrophies damagingly when it is not. In the famous opening passage that reminds us how the very thoughts we have dismissed because they are our own "come back to us with a certain alienated majesty" when spoken by another, Emerson describes self-reliance as the apperceptive capacity for recognizing our elusive, divine selves: "A man should learn to detect and watch that gleam of light which flashes across his mind from within, more than the lustre of the firmament of bards and sages" (W, II, 45). Self-reliance is a power unique and new to each person, "and none but he knows what that is which he can do, *nor does he know until he has tried*" (W, II, 46; my emphasis). Ultimately selfhood and self-reliance are both confirmed and brought about by the same effort: *Being* a reliant self *makes* you one, for "with the exercise of self-trust new powers shall appear" (W, II, 76). Always, the stakes are the obliteration or the strengthening of the faculties, the disabling or the enabling of power. Any act that "takes away the presentiments," as does the habit of moral oppression, or that takes one away from one's spirits in prison impairs this faculty of openness. Such acts obstruct that openness without which the relation that is the self and the reliance that is its activity cannot occur. Self-reliance, then, requires the same demanding openness that compensation, too, required. Self-reliance and compensation require, respectively, an openness that obeys the commands of an allowed relation and that submits to the Orphic asceticism of adequate desire.

To have arrived yet again at the concept of openness in our investigation of Emerson's affirmations and of the ways he meets the risks they entail is to have arrived "not at a wall, but at interminable oceans," as Emerson wryly describes such argumentative terminals in "Experience" (W, III, 73). Of course, it is not at all surprising that the affirmation of two so closely related principles as self-reliance and compensation should entail, each in its own way, the same kind of risk—that of openness. Since the risks of affirmation are rhetorical as well as substantive or moral, the openness that self-reliance and compensation require of their adherents has a rhetorical counterpart in what articulating these principles requires of their affirmer. Before leaving self-reliance, as text and principle, it will be useful to pause over these rhetorical demands and Emerson's response to them.

Rhetorically speaking, the openness Emerson's principles require is that argumentative reversal I described in Chapter I as the climactic opening and the initiative ending. In such a form, announcement takes the place of conclusiveness, whereas collocation of instances takes the place of proof; and postponement becomes the technique whereby the end of a lecture, or essay, or passage acquires its initiative (as distinct from persuasive) momentum. Such a form is "always complete but never finished." [21] Such a form does not merely lack closure. It is constructed to accommodate both additions and deletions. To the reader who expects progress toward closure instead of indefinite postponement of closure (not to say the precluding of closure), such a form seems haphazard, inconsistent, or simply absent. But the absence of closure, or rather the displacement of closure from final to opening climax, is itself a technique. It is the rhetorical counterpart to Emersonian openness, or divination, or Orphic asceticism, and Emerson takes its technical demands as seriously as he does its moral ones. His frequent self-deprecating or self-protecting asides about the supposedly ineffective or unconventional progress of his arguments should not be taken as apology. They should be taken as indications that Emerson is aware of the rhetorical as well as the moral burdens his message imposes and as indications that this burden lies with the reader as much as it does with Emerson. Moreover, they should be taken as confirm-

21. The phrase was an advertisement for the Globe-Wernicke sectional bookcase popular in 1890s America. John Kouwenhoven quotes it in his stimulating discussion of open form in "What's 'American' about America," an essay in his collection, *The Beer Can by the Highway* (Garden City, N.Y., 1961), 49–50.

ing correspondences between the burdens of message and those of form.

"Self-Reliance" characterizes succinctly what it is about Emerson's message that resists articulation: "This one fact the world hates; that the soul *becomes*. . . . Why then do we prate of self-reliance? In as much as the soul is present there will be power not confident [that is, not needing to rely] but agent [that is, directly active]" (W, II, 69). Because the Emersonian quest is undertaken within certainty and not toward certainty, it is in constant danger of being obviated by its own legitimacy. It is a quest doomed to succeed.

A little less than a third of the way through "Self-Reliance" Emerson says of his topic that "the highest truth on this subject remains unsaid; probably cannot be said" (W, I, 68). Yet only two paragraphs and as many pages later, he gives this opposite assessment of his topic and the articulation it has permitted: "This is the ultimate fact which we so quickly reach on this, as on every topic, the resolution of all into the ever-blessed ONE" (W, I, 70). The contradiction between these two assessments is instructive. If the first is a complaint or a recognition that articulation must fail before the ineffable, the second must be an exultation that the "highest truth," which "probably cannot be said," was reached after all. Yet Emerson's second assessment does not sound like exultation or relief. It sounds like regret, and it sounds enervated. At the same time, the first assessment sounds energetic and hopeful despite its ostensible helplessness.

The predicament is not just the poet's age-old lament that the form that communicates is also the letter that killeth. Emerson's particular plaint does not just concern ineffability in general; it concerns that fact of becoming which, he knows, the world hates. Emerson wants to make the world love that fact. In order to affirm the power he sees this fact as ensuring, he must reverse the world's disinclination to believe in this fluidity and to submit to it. The quest within a certainty about flux is a quest in which arriving at the goal becomes problematical. When "Circles" says that "the coming only is sacred" (W, II, 319), it is not of course arrival but becoming that is meant. Arrival is not the culmination but the doom of the Emersonian quest, for in the Emersonian quest the goal functions to give direction but never to invite closure. Thus Emerson's rhetorical aim is never to arrive at a wall but always at interminable oceans. His message—the despised truth "that the soul *becomes*"—constantly places his form in the predicament of needing to avoid closure. A related characteristic of Emerson's problematical message is its insistence on newness, on youth, on originality.

The volume's opening essay, "History," ends by announcing this theme of newness. Since the essay as a whole has been about history as the record of the works of the one mind—the Over-Soul—it is not surprising that its final paragraph accomplishes its announcement about newness in terms of the sort of recording, the sort of written articulation, this newness requires: "Broader and deeper we must write our annals,—from an influx of the ever new, ever sanative conscience,—if we would trulier express our central and wide-related nature, instead of the old chronology of selfishness and pride to which we have too long lent our eyes" (W, I, 40). Openness to this "ever new, ever sanative conscience" is not here the desired result of reading. It is the necessary condition for making available those rare thoughts which, "The Over-Soul" says, "always find us young and keep us so" (W, II, 272). To be kept young by what can only find you if you manage to *be* young, you must be devoted to that hated fact—the fact that the soul becomes. Despising this fact may be the way of the world, but becoming strong enough to honor and welcome it is precisely the *via negativa* that Emerson describes in "Self-Reliance" as his "nearest approach" to that ineffable "highest truth on the subject," before which he has pretended the essay must perforce falter. Here is the description:

When good is near you, when you have life in yourself, it is not by any known way; you shall not discern the footprints of another; you shall not see the face of man; you shall not hear any name;—the way, the thought, the good, shall be wholly strange and new. It shall exclude example and experience. You take the way from man, not to man. All persons that ever existed are its forgotten ministers. Fear and hope are alike beneath it. (W, I, 68–69)

Emerson's argument is here attempting what it is describing: an approach. That approach is a *via negativa* because its direction is not *to* but *from*, and because Emerson must use emphatic negatives to describe its dire uniqueness. As long as Emerson can use such negative description to adumbrate what he is affirming, it can remain a way, a becoming, and not an arrival. But soon the truth burns through the adumbration, and Emerson is left with the problem of arrival at "that ultimate fact which we so quickly reach on this, as on every topic." It may be debated whether this two-paragraph passage of avowed incapacity, attempted approach, and regrettably successful attainment weakens or strengthens the essay that is but two-thirds finished when it occurs. Either way, the passage exemplifies Emerson's consciousness of the rhetorical problems entailed by his message of newness and becoming.

Emerson presents overtly his search for a way to affirm self-reliance so that he can present it as a struggle. Invoking Yeats's celebrated formulation that "from the struggle with others we make rhetoric, from the struggle with ourselves we make poetry," Matthiessen stimulatingly observes that Emerson (and Whitman) blurred that distinction.[22] I would add that Emerson (and Whitman) elided not only the struggle with self and with others but also a third struggle—the struggle with subject matter. The struggle for postponement that Emerson's subject of continuous becoming imposed upon him was a struggle to keep the wound open. It was as painful as it was "sanative," and the correspondence between the rhetorical and the moral openness required was a correspondence that emphasized the cost of newness while it confirmed the power of newness.

Always, Emerson sought and counseled what *Nature* called "original relation." By "original relation" Emerson meant not just individual perception of one's unique place and function, but also a new kind of telling, a relating that would originate.

22. Matthiessen, *American Renaissance*, 23.

For this kind of originating eloquence it was necessary to read and write the universe. Emerson cherished the principle of compensation for enduring in the universe. He saw self-reliance as required for prevailing in the universe. He found correspondence fundamental to reading and writing the universe. In order to study the demands of this enabling correspondence, it is necessary to turn attention now to *Nature*.

V

"Original Relation": *Nature* and Correspondence

Nothing but God is self-dependent. (EL, II, 17)

Men fancy they are pendants to the universe & lo! All the time the universe is pendant to them. (JMN, VIII, 410)

And in common life whosoever has seen a person of powerful character and happy genius, will have re-marked how easily he took all things with him—the persons, the opinions, and the day, and nature became ancillary to a man. (Nature, W, I, 22; CW, I, 16)

 ature is clearly a work of genius, whether one understands *genius* to mean a revolutionary spirit or a prevailing one, an exceptional talent or an individual bent. To me, *Nature* is a work of genius in all these senses. An unsettling combination of treatise and meditation, Emerson's first book is at once didactic, as though being proclaimed by some tutelary emissary, and musing, as though it is an almost involuntary utterance. Unsettlingly original though it is, *Nature* (1836) belongs with other manifestoes of its period. Like Shelley's *Defence of Poetry* (written in 1821 though not published until 1840), *Nature* assigns to poetry the most responsible and revolutionary role, and does so in a curiously valedictory way. Following Coleridge, *Nature* repeatedly separates the immediate and synthesizing power of reason from understanding's more dependent functioning and merely analytical capacity.[1] Like Words-

---

1. On the evolution of Emerson's use of reason from "icy reason" in an early poem to reason as a higher moral faculty (in 1834), see CW, I, xxii. See also Robert E. Spiller, "Ralph Waldo Emerson," in *Literary History of the United States*, ed. Robert E. Spiller, *et al.* (Rev. ed.; New York, 1953), 370, on the importance in *Nature* of the Coleridgean distinction between reason and understanding.

worth's *Preface* and like the *Communist Manifesto* of Marx and Engels, *Nature* seeks to challenge and to define "the spirit of the age," as Wordsworth calls it.[2] And like Blake's *Marriage of Heaven and Hell*, *Nature*'s commitments and convictions characterize its author, but in a form that its author will never repeat.

Perhaps more than originality or genius or conviction, audacity is the most accurate word for the achievement and the effect of *Nature*. As a first instance of *Nature*'s audacity, take Emerson's description of a January sunset in his third chapter, "Beauty." After sketching in the shapes and tints of the sky and specifying the live, sweet quality of the air, Emerson says that it would take the songs of Homer or Shakespeare to "re-form for me in words" the "meaning in the live repose of the valley behind the mill." Then he goes right on to describe the scene, "re-forming it in words" most eloquently indeed, though not, it is true, reading or translating the scene before him. I quote the whole passage:

> The western clouds divided and subdivided themselves into pink flakes modulated with tints of unspeakable softness; and the air had so much life and sweetness, that it was a pain to come within doors. What was it that nature would say? Was there no meaning in the live repose of the valley behind the mill, and which Homer or Shakespeare could not re-form for me in words? The leafless trees became spires of flame in the sunset, with the blue east for their background, and the stars of the dead calices of flowers, and every withered stem and stubble rimed with frost, contribute something to the mute music. (W, I, 17–18; CW, I, 13–14)[3]

Invoking the names of the two greatest Western poets has not intimidated Emerson or induced modesty—false or otherwise. Neither does invoking the names of other thinkers, Western or Eastern, who have worked on the momentous question that *Na-*

2. The *Communist Manifesto* was first published in 1848 and first appeared in English translation in 1850.

3. The CW editors point out that a parallel passage may be found in JMN, IV, 379–80.

ture addresses, the question of the relation of mind and matter. In "Language" Emerson calls this question "the standing problem which has exercised the wonder and study of every fine genius since the world began." He then goes on to list the company he unaffectedly and undauntedly feels that he keeps: Pythagoras, Plato, Bacon, Leibnitz, Swedenborg, as well as unspecified thinkers "from the era of the Egyptians and Brahmins" (W, I, 34; CW, I, 22).

Another catalog, this one of topics, provides a third instance of Emerson's bold confidence. In his "Introduction" he lists as follows the phenomena that resist elucidation by unworthy theories or world-conceptions, but that yield to worthy ones: "Language, sleep, madness, dreams, beasts, sex" (W, I, 4; CW, I, 8). It is an arresting catalog, certainly. Death is notably missing from the list, unless sleep counts for both. Since language is listed first, perhaps this list of the unexplained and allegedly inexplicable is a list of sign systems, a possibility that would account for the initially startling presence of madness.[4] If the list does concern various sign systems, the function of beasts, which is far from immediately obvious, might then be to test or exemplify. But what of sex? What is its place in this list? Indeed, what is meant by sex? Passion, reproduction, the anatomical division into genders? Someone might regard the juxtaposition of beasts and sex, and the sequence from dreams to sex (or from madness, or even from sleep) as evidence that Emerson thinks sex is bestial or an aberration or both. Fortunately our present interest in the list is not in the secrets of its parataxis, but in its bold denomination of six topics that still today remain mysteries in the sense of being things about which there is always more to be known. The boldness of the list lies in its implication—clear from the full context—that here Emerson is introducing a theory of nature, or a theory of the relation between mind and matter, that addresses abiding mysteries like those listed. For the affirming Emerson, the hitherto unexplained and allegedly inexplicable will radiate meaning and invite interpretation once the right reader comes

4. Originally the word *madness* was omitted. But the 1849 edition added it, and it has been retained by all subsequent editions, including CW, I, 286.

along, because "undoubtedly we have no questions to ask which are unanswerable" (W, I, 3; CW, I, 7).

Throughout *Nature*, questioning is an important activity, and Emerson's use of the interrogative form contributes to his book's bold, buoyant, and forceful effect. The book's opening paragraph is virtually composed of questions: "Why should not we also enjoy an original relation to the universe? Why should not we have a poetry and philosophy of insight and not of tradition, and a religion by revelation to us, and not the history of theirs? . . . Why should we grope among the dry bones of the past?" And his second paragraph summarizes and introduces the book's entire project this way: "Let us *interrogate* the great apparition that shines so peacefully around us. Let us *inquire*, to what end is nature?" (W, I, 4; CW, I, 7; my emphasis). Emerson seems to allow himself a faintly quizzical diction in those sentences of ostensible promise. "The great apparition that shines so peacefully around us": There seems a hint of caricature in that appelation, a hint of reproach in the clause that attributes peacefulness to this apparition as though an apparition ought to disturb nature more. Similarly, to speak of interrogating such a presence seems to direct more than a hint of caricature at the questioner—at Emerson, or at ourselves. The diction implies that one's interrogations may be inappropriately formulated or that one's hope of an answer may be misplaced, considering the addressee's blissful impassivity. To address one's questions to nature may mean encountering the riddling Sphinx.[5] Such an encounter, as Emerson's poem "The Sphinx" richly dramatizes, puts the burden on the interrogator, not on the oracle. In his note to "The Sphinx," Edward Emerson quotes a passage from an 1859 notebook that summarizes how completely the value of riddling depends on the interrogator and how questioning can bring madness at least as readily as it may bring revelation. (That reference to madness glosses as well the presence of madness in the list of topics we just examined.) "But if the mind lives only in particulars, and see only differences (wanting the power to see the whole—all in

5. The "Language" chapter makes the comparison explicitly. See W, I, 34; CW, I, 22.

each), then the world addresses to this mind a question it cannot answer, and each new fact tears it in pieces, and it is vanquished by the distracting variety" (W, IX, 412).

However extensively Emerson's diction qualifies the promise that *Nature*'s opening questions hold out and qualifies also the faith in questioning that *Nature*'s second paragraph declares, the question itself remains entirely serious and entirely characteristic in its audacious sweep and simplicity. "To what end is nature?" The articulation of the answer proper comes a little more than halfway through the book, in the chapter "Idealism." "Nature is made to conspire with spirit to emancipate us" (W, I, 50; CW, I, 30). As we saw in the discussion of "Experience," the bond from which we are to be emancipated is none other than nature itself.[6] To what end is nature, then? To the end of its own destruction, destruction in service of liberation. The more we make nature disappear the more we use nature for the designated end. "Nature is thoroughly mediate. It is made to serve" (W, I, 40; CW, I, 25). If Emerson were a lesser poet and a lesser human being, this situation would scarcely be bittersweet, let alone paradoxical. As it is, however, the particular medal of Jove whose one side is ME and whose other side is NOT-ME is the coin of a realm that Emerson holds in an awe approaching wariness, a realm where Emerson fears to be too much at home even as he scorns being an alien there. That realm is "the Ideal."

Emerson's attitude toward idealism and the ideal is one of his most attractive as well as characteristic traits. The best summary of it is in Oscar W. Firkins' estimable literary biography of Emerson: "Was Emerson an idealist? A distinction is imperative. In the sense of a disbeliever in the actuality of matter, Emerson was no convinced or committed idealist. . . . He liked matter, and its conversion into pure spirit would perhaps have affected him as unpleasantly as the proposal to convert a tried and faithful dog into a human being." Though Emerson was not an idealist in the sense of being against matter, "In the sense of one who maintains the absolute dependence of sense-impressions on character and intelligence, he was perhaps the most sweeping, the most fear-

6. See Chapter II, p. 60, herein.

less, the most insistent idealist that ever lived. . . . Emerson is tireless in descanting on the fulness and precision of this authority [that is, the authority of character and intelligence]. To abolish matter is needless; its enslavement will suffice."[7] The enslavement of matter by spirit will suffice, as Firkins says, and it will constitute precisely the reverse of the situation experienced by the sensuous man of "unrenewed understanding." "To the senses and the unrenewed understanding, belongs a sort of instinctive belief in the absolute existence of nature. In their view, mind and nature are indissolubly joined" (W, I, 49; CW, I, 30). Thus, doubting the absolute, independent existence of nature is a "noble doubt" and not necessarily a madness, though Emerson remains emphatic about the risks to sanity and the affronts to felicity of overdoing this noble doubt.

Near the end of the "Idealism" chapter Emerson shifts the debate away from technical contests as to whether matter is as real as spirit and centers it instead on the advantage of an idealist position over a materialist one. The advantage of attributing reality to spirit and not to matter is that this view turns out to be more inclusive, not less. Only the best minds are able to entertain the noble doubt that matter may be phenomenal rather than substantial. Those are precisely the minds that know how to question "the great apparition that shines so peacefully around us." Moreover, they are the minds to whom that great apparition's "distracting variety" addresses a text to be interpreted rather than "a question it cannot answer." Those are the philosophical and poetic minds. Only to those minds is nature the NOT-ME, because only to those minds is "the universe . . . composed of Nature and the Soul" as separate and separable entities (W, I, 4; CW, I, 8) rather than as entities that are "indissolubly joined" (W, I, 49; CW, I, 30).

Emerson introduces his definition of nature as the NOT-ME by stipulating that it is a philosophical definition, not a common one. Far from being naïve or inadequate, that definition of Emerson's title term takes into account more complexities than it seems to and accomplishes precisely what Emerson wants it to

7. Firkins, *Ralph Waldo Emerson*, 343–44.

accomplish.[8] By defining nature as the NOT-ME Emerson divides not only all creation but all that is conceivable into two parts: ME and NOT-ME. Since the definition involves a distinction—that between ME and NOT-ME—both terms are equally important. By referring to a NOT-ME, Emerson of course purports to assume that one knows what ME is. Elsewhere in *Nature*, however, Emerson provides a definition of ideas that constitutes at the same time a definition of the ME. Emerson's definition of ideas may be taken as a definition of the ME (or of soul, spirit, mind, or maker), because these terms are interchangeable in Emerson when they are being opposed to their equally interchangeable counterparts—NOT-ME, world, matter, body, or made. We may postpone further attention to this interchangeability for now and proceed at once to Emerson's definition of ideas.

It comes as part of his discussion of the noble doubt. The noble doubt is valuable, because it "fastens the attention upon immortal necessary uncreated natures, that is upon Ideas" (W, I, 56; CW, I, 34). "Immortal, necessary, uncreated." Though it is implicit and adjectival rather than explicit and nominalized, this grouping of epithets constitutes a definition of ideas (or the ME) as clearly as Emerson's famous sentence about the NOT-ME constitutes a definition of nature. Latter-day readers, who have Emerson's entire published work to teach them, are in a much better position to comprehend the equation that this list of epithets constitutes than *Nature*'s first audience was. No wonder they found Emerson's first book demanding, queer, and cryptic.[9] The queerest features of this list are the homely, stipulative neologism *uncreated* and the startling presence of the word *necessary*. Putting *necessary* after *immortal* in his definition of ideas serves Emerson in two opposite ways at once. It makes *necessary* honorific so that its sense of *indispensable* operates. Yet its sense of *unavoidable* continues to operate as well, because immortality

8. In contrast to the argument I shall be developing, Porte, *Representative Man*, 225, finds Emerson's definition "simplistic and naïve" and says that "Emerson himself sensed that this was the case."

9. A convenient collection of contemporary estimates of *Nature* is in Merton M. Sealts, Jr., and Alfred R. Ferguson (eds.), *Emerson's* Nature—*Origin, Growth, Meaning* (New York and Toronto, 1969), 81–110.

concerns death, no matter how positive the association may be. Consequently, *necessary* both borrows semantic positiveness from the ideas of liberation and glory associated with immortality and also lends to *immortality* some of its own dire associations with inevitability and coercion, thereby preventing the glib or dogmatic responses that *immortal* could arouse and inviting more actively individual ones instead.

Uncreated, the third in this group of three equivalents, is the only word not in common currency, though all three words are virtually redefined by their collocation here. By the time *uncreated* follows *necessary*, the idea of immortality has shed associations of fame and of easy or miraculous or elected survival. It has taken on the austere promise that everywhere characterizes Emerson's *Nature*, as it does his affirmations generally. How does this third epithet, *uncreated*, complete this addition of austerity to the promise and celebration that might have been too automatic if *immortal* had been allowed to stand alone? By being a past participle, by being an opposite, and by being a negative. As a past participle *uncreated* raises the question, however remotely: Not-created by what agent? As an opposite, it is a word about life and creation, not about death and mortality. And as a negative, it echoes *immortal* even while opposing it semantically, for like *immortal*, *uncreated* denominates by alleging that a known quantity is absent. Between these symmetrical outside terms, *necessary* makes a suggestive inside term indeed, and the entire grouping constitutes an arresting triptych of equivalents for those special "natures" called ideas. I have described and analyzed this triptych because I find it appealing in itself, because I hear in it the blend of threat and promise that Emerson's affirming and confirming voices make, and because I connect its implicit definition with the much more explicit one in the book's "Introduction"—Emerson's definition of his title term, *nature*, as the NOT-ME.

THE PROJECT of defining his title term should have been intimidating to Emerson, but he executes it with the same unaffected audacity that typifies his whole book. "Nature is perhaps the most complex word in the language." So much so that "any full history of the uses of nature would be a history of a large part of human thought." So writes Raymond Williams in his collection of synopses, *Keywords*. The synopsis for each "keyword" details the changing usages Williams finds particularly revealing of certain cultural changes.[10] Because his entry for *nature* helps to place Emerson's definition of *nature* as the NOT-ME, "that is, both nature and art, all other men and my own body," some exposition of Williams' findings about the history of the word's usage is in order.

Williams distinguishes three senses: In the first sense, *nature* means "the essential character and quality of something," as in a sentence like "It was her nature to be impatient." In this sense *nature* is a "specific singular," describing "a quality . . . immediately defined by a specific reference." In contrast, sense two and sense three are usually "abstract singulars." That is, in the second sense *nature* refers to "the inherent force which directs the world or human beings or both," while in the third sense *nature* denotes "the material world itself taken as including or not including human beings."

The more abstract sense of *nature* as formative force (sense two) and *nature* as existing creation (sense three) evolved by a process "structurally and historically cognate with the emergence of *God* from *a god* or *the gods*." When a once-specific noun becomes abstract, universalized, and institutionalized in this way, striking changes in thought and attitudes are both attested and permitted. Such a change from particular to universal allows greater flexibility of meaning, but it also allows greater manipulation of those meanings and *by* them.[11]

In any case, Emerson used *nature* in all three senses throughout his work. His definition of *nature* as the NOT-ME is a sense three definition. Here are the well-known lines:

10. Raymond Williams, *Keywords: A Vocabulary of Culture and Society* (Oxford, 1976), 184–89. All quotations from *Keywords* below can be found in this five-page synopsis unless otherwise indicated.

11. Williams' most instructive discussion of this development is in his introduction to *Culture and Society, 1780–1950* (New York and London, 1958). There he traces the development of the five words *industry, democracy, class, art,* and *culture.*

Philosophically considered, the universe is composed of Nature and the Soul. Strictly speaking, therefore, all that is separate from us, all which Philosophy distinguishes as the NOT ME, that is, both nature and art, all other men and my own body, must be ranked under this name, NATURE. In enumerating the values of nature and casting up their sum, I shall use the word in both senses;—in its common and in its philosophical import. (W, I, 4; CW, I, 8)

Two monosyllables—albeit uppercase ones—suffice to stipulate what Emerson will use *nature* to refer to. *Nature* will refer to "the NOT ME." More audaciously still, this definition of *nature* covers, says Emerson, both senses in which he will use it, the philosophical sense that distinguishes self from circumstance, and the common sense that "refers to essences unchanged by man; space, the air, the river, the leaf" (W, I, 5; CW, I, 8). Conflating common and philosophical uses of *nature* presents no difficulty, Emerson assures us: "In inquiries so general as our present one, the inaccuracy is not material; no confusion of thought will occur." Why is it unnecessary to insist on the common (*i.e.,* Romantic) distinction between art and nature which reserves *nature* for designating only materials that have remained unmixed with human will? Because such operations of the human will "taken together are so insignificant." Those operations do not signify; they do not constitute signs; "in an impression so grand as that of the world on the human mind, they do not vary the result" and so need not have a separate designation among all that is NOT-ME. In addition, all that is NOT-ME is clearly outside of me, whether mixed or unmixed with human will.

Like others of his time, Emerson concentrates, in this definition, on Williams' sense three—nature as the created, and he omits from consideration the idea of nature as formative force (Williams' sense two, or what Emerson himself elsewhere terms *natura naturans*).[12] But in one important respect, Emerson's definition does not exemplify Williams' findings. It does not lead to

12. Paul Lauter has detailed these usages of Emerson in "Truth and Nature: Emerson's Use of Two Complex Words," *English Literary History*, 27, 1 (1960), 66–85, especially 79–85, where Lauter quotes from Emerson's "Nature."

either of the ramifications that Williams describes. According to Williams, two related changes occurred when, in the eighteenth and nineteenth centuries, the idea of nature as an inherent and shaping force gave way to the idea of nature as the material world. First, the Enlightenment's emphasis on discoverable laws of nature "led to a common identification of Nature with Reason: the object of observation with the mode of observation." Second, this "provided for a significant variation," which may be associated with the Romantic movement, whereby "nature was contrasted with what had been made of man, or what man had made of himself. A 'state of nature' could be contrasted—sometimes pessimistically but more often optimistically and even programmatically—with an existing state of society." Pointing out that since the last third of the eighteenth century "one of the most powerful uses of NATURE has been in this selective sense of goodness and innocence," Williams summarizes that use of *nature* by saying that it is "what man had not made, though if he made it long enough ago—a hedgerow or a desert—it will usually be included as natural." Does Emerson's emphasis on nature as creat*ed* rather than creat*ing* lead him to identify nature with reason? Obviously not. Obviously Emerson's definition of nature as the NOT-ME does not ramify along those characteristically Enlightenment lines, for in calling nature the NOT-ME Emerson makes the ME opposite to nature. Since his entire treatise makes it plain repeatedly that reason belongs to this ME, it is clear that Emerson is not identifying reason and nature, but rather opposing them.

If Emerson's emphasis on nature as creat*ed* rather than creat*ing* does not lead him to the Enlightenment position that Williams describes, does it lead him to the Romantic variation whereby "nature was contrasted with what had been made of man, or what man had made of himself?" Once again the answer is no. Though Emerson looks to nature for instruction, comfort, stimulation, even inspiration—in *Nature* and throughout his works—he is careful to stipulate in his "Introduction" that the definition of his title term excludes a contrast between man-made and otherwise-made. That contrast Emerson calls immaterial to his purposes. He has sweepingly set aside a distinction that a lesser writer might belabor.

Emerson's emphasis on sense three yields neither the characteristically Enlightenment ramifications nor the characteristically Romantic ones that Williams identifies. The distinction between NOT-ME and ME does not entail a division within the created, nor does it make an alliance between two orders of the created. Instead, the distinction between NOT-ME and ME discriminates between the created and the *un*created. Absent from Williams' synopsis, this discrimination is the most important one in all Emerson. Given the Emersonian habit of beginning climactically, it is fitting that the critical distinction between created and uncreated should spring full-blown from his first book—indeed, from a stipulative definition to the title term in the introductory section of his first book.

IN EMPHASIZING the freshness of Emerson's terminology I have perhaps seemed to ignore that Emerson's distinction between ME and NOT-ME belongs to the tradition of post-Kantian metaphysics that arranges the universe so as to accommodate individual authority without doing away with divine wisdom.[13] I have perhaps also seemed to ignore that Carlyle used the terms ME and NOT-ME in *Sartor Resartus* (for the 1836 Boston edition of which Emerson wrote an introduction), that the terms were Carlyle's translation of Johann Gottlieb Fichte's *das Nicht-Ich*, and that the whole distinction between self as consciousness and world as phenomenon was current and pervasive in the German idealism to which Carlyle had led Emerson.[14] In describing Emerson's

13. Robert E. Spiller's introduction to CW, I, provides a clear overview showing the revolt against Calvinism that led Emerson to search out a new philosophy, the various texts and authors Emerson borrowed from, and the way not only *Nature* but the two major addresses—"American Scholar" and "Divinity School" —stand (with, of course, their supporting lectures and journal passages) as the articulation of the "First Philosophy" that Emerson arrived at. See note 1, above.

14. See Stephen E. Whicher's note in his *Selections From Ralph Waldo Emerson: An Organic Anthology* (Boston, 1957), 472; see also Carlyle's *Sartor Resartus*, ed. Charles Frederick Harrold (New York, 1937), especially p. 170, n. 4, and Harrold's introduction, xi ff.

brand of this idealism as fresh and audacious I mean to stress that he has appropriated a tradition, not to assert that he has founded one. He used this tradition in at least three characteristic and important ways. First, he used it to insist on the creativity of the ME as attested by the made-ness of the NOT-ME. Second, Emerson's semiotics are appropriated from the tradition's teaching that nature is the text of spirit. Third, Emerson's vitalism is a more drastic version of the tradition's teaching that dialectical process avoids or destroys dogmatic stagnation. A further word now about the monosyllables ME and NOT-ME before turning to Emerson's semiotics and his vitalism.

Since Emerson's distinction does indeed belong to a far from obscure tradition, more familiar terms than ME and NOT-ME exist for it. Coleridge's *reason* and *understanding* are cognate; and Emerson himself, of course, adopts these explicitly. He also adopts cognate terms that are more generally used: such psycho-theological vocabulary as *self* and *world*, *spirit* and *matter*, *mind* and *matter*, *ideal* and *real*, *God* and *creation*, or *cause* and *effect*. The familiarity of most of these terms, the extensive explication available for those that, like Coleridge's, are technical, and the fact that Emerson's kind of distinction belongs to a tradition—all these considerations may make it seem as if the terms ME and NOT-ME should be assimilated to those other terms. Actually, however, the cognate terms I just listed will themselves suggest the special properties of the less-familiar monosyllables and my reasons for dwelling on Emerson's adoption of them.

First, the pairs in that list are either confusingly technical or confusingly imprecise. Second, Emerson's terminology solves the problem of whether one is distinguishing orders of perception, orders of being, or orders of action, whereas all the paired terms on the list leave this unsettled. Some of the pairs would normally be taken as distinguishing between two kinds of perceptual capacity—Coleridge's reason and understanding, for example; some as distinguishing two ontological categories, like self and world; and some as distinguishing between purposive action and its consequences, or between design that is intentional and design that is merely discerned—cause and effect, for instance.

Worst of all, at least one pair from the list would normally be taken to refer to any of these three ways of making Emerson's distinction—mind and matter. Mind and matter might distinguish the succumbing of the latter to the former, or the general qualities of the one from those of the other, or the specific perceptual capacity of each.

Emerson's choice of the less familiar ME and NOT-ME avoids every one of these confusions or these needs for expert, technical exposition. Astonishingly, we know what they mean. How is this astonishing intelligibility managed? By reversing the simple pedagogical and rhetorical strategy of using the known to define the unknown. This is a deeply Emersonian reversal.

In defining nature as that which is NOT-ME, Emerson assumes that we know what is ME. He puts the allegedly unknown in the rhetorical and grammatical position of the known, and thus confers knowledge by attributing it. Emerson's *uncreated* works in a similar way: it too stipulates the absent quality as the definitive one. Whereas the formulation NOT-ME uses a relatively esoteric term as its reference point, however, the word *uncreated* does not. *Uncreated* is the negation of *created*, a relatively exoteric word. Consequently, while speaking of a NOT-ME fosters the heady assumption that one knows what ME is, speaking of an uncreated removes the limiting assumption that only a created can be spoken of as real. Both negatives make a special point of the absence by which they are characterizing their referent. This designating by absence or naming by negation confers a quality of being unnameable in any more direct way. In her book on paradox, Rosalie Colie summarizes the characteristics and advantages of negative affirmation:

> The appropriate way to express transcendent deity is by tautology (*e.g.*, God's own self-referential comment to Moses, "I am that I am") or by negative affirmations which are by definition paradoxical (*e.g.*, God is incomprehensible, or infinite). That is, there are two ways of avoiding contamination of the divine essence by implications carried in metaphors from human experience, the one, to use terms of totality, the

other, to use negative or "ablative" terms (Infinity, Eternity, Immutability).[15]

Emerson's 1835 Journal, which is designated "RO Mind" by the JMN editors, is devoted to distinguishing reason from understanding and is thus clearly part of Emerson's preparation for *Nature*. It contains the following cancelled fragment: "That I may not seem to confound what I adore with anything unworthy let me further define and describe" (JMN, V, 271, and n. 8). The fragment reveals Emerson's wish to avoid the contamination by language that Colie speaks of and yet to use language to signify and celebrate the ineffable. The combination of hope and fear in that wish are responsible for *Nature*'s organization, language, and tone.

To make a special point of the absence of ME when designating nature as the NOT-ME is to stress neither nature's reality nor its unreality, its cyclical recurrence or its mutability, its beauty or its crudity. All these characteristics of nature interested Emerson, all were available to his imagination, and all figure in his book to varying extents. But none of these is for Emerson the critical, identifying characteristic of nature. That essential trait he can specify only by negation. He can specify it only as an absence or a difference. Similarly, the critical, identifying characteristic of the ME (or spirit, or Over-Soul, or ideas) is neither its individuality nor its universality, its supremacy or its subtlety, its reliability or its elusiveness. All these figure in Emerson's work to varying degrees, but none is the identifying characteristic. That function is reserved for the concept that "spirit creates" (W, I, 63; CW, I, 38). Instead of being creat*ed*, spirit is creat*ive*. "Spirit creates" is Emerson's positive version of the stipulation in the "Idealism" chapter that ideas are uncreated. The mode of that creating is as important as the fact of it, yet the "Idealism" chapter does not tell about this mode. All idealism can do is act as "a hypothesis to account for nature by other principles than those of carpentry and chemistry." Idealism can*not* "account for that

15. Rosalie Colie, *Paradoxia Epidemica: The Renaissance Tradition of Paradox* (Princeton, 1966), 24; see also chapters 4, 5, and 6, *ibid.*

consanguinity which we acknowledge to [nature]" (W, I, 63; CW, I, 38). That is, "Idealism" is a pivotal chapter in *Nature* because idealism can serve "to apprise us of the eternal *distinction* between soul and the world" (W, I, 63; CW, I, 38; my emphasis) but not of the *connection*, "the consanguinity" between those distinct entities. Resemblance or correspondence is, of course, that connection.

"Identity is the vanishing point of resemblance," Wallace Stevens wrote. In emphasizing the separation between nature and spirit or matter and mind, Emerson was also emphasizing their resemblance. Indeed, his purpose in denying their identity was to assert their similitude. That relationship of resemblance is correspondence. The remainder of this chapter deals with Emerson's affirmation of correspondence and with the confirming costs peculiar to its inherent dynamism. Emersonian correspondence is dynamic to the point of volatility. So little is correspondence a static relationship that it threatens constantly to be an unstable one. This threatening volatility of correspondence is, I shall argue, the cost of its regenerative vitality.

EMERSON'S OWN term for the correspondence that he celebrated and urged was "original relation." As I suggested at the end of Chapter IV, he meant by this phrase not only an aboriginal sense of the immediacy of divinity that ought to be revived, but also an originality of response that ought to be cultivated and an expression or way of telling that must itself be originating, or empowering. Emersonian correspondence is a sign-system, a code—a code to be deciphered and a code of behavior as well. Sherman Paul, whose entire study of Emerson is devoted to Emerson's uses and versions of correspondence, observes that for Emerson "nature was instrumental both as the activator of insight and as the object of focus. Correspondence, therefore, as an inspirational means *was sympathy with nature, as well as the doctrine of its expression.*" [16] Paul emphasizes this "sympathetic" version of correspondence because for Emerson correspondence did not

16. Sherman Paul, *Emerson's Angle of Vision: Man and Nature in American Experience* (Cambridge, Mass., 1952), 87; my emphasis.

just declare that nature matched spirit, as Swedenborgian correspondence did. For Emerson correspondence was more dynamic
than that; it both required and enabled a perceiving consciousness to experience it.[17]

The dynamics of correspondence that Paul describes when he
says that nature could both activate insight and serve "as the object of focus," Albert Gelpi describes in another way. Following
Perry Miller, Gelpi describes Emerson as blurring the distinction
between types and tropes.[18] His insight is based on Miller's account of how Jonathan Edwards tried to reinstate typology as a
way to make religious use of post-Newtonian nature, in a canny
if unsuccessful attempt to prevent science from killing religion.[19]
Typology, or seeing natural events as signs of spiritual intention
in the way that Old Testament events had been interpreted as
prefiguring New Testament events, was one way of using the
natural world to preach about the supernatural. The other was
tropological allegorization whereby a social or natural circumstance—the more homely and recognizable the better—provided an analogue, fable, or parable for some ethical or moral
preachment. In the tradition of Jonathan Edwards and Edward
Taylor, Gelpi points out, Emerson regarded nature as a type of
spirit—that is, as a sign indicating the existence and especially
the intention of spirit. But Emerson did not distinguish between
nature as type or adumbration of spirit and nature as trope or
analogy for spirit. Gelpi writes: "If it is true that 'the universe is
the externization of the soul' [W, III, 14] it was often not clear
*whether Emerson was referring to his soul or to the Over-Soul,
or whether he would have wanted to make such distinctions.*"[20]
This lack of clarity is very important: Emerson would *not* have
wanted, did not want, to make distinctions between his soul and
the Over-Soul. So completely did he wish the Over-Soul and the

17. *Ibid.*, 4, 62−65, and *passim*.
18. Albert Gelpi, *The Tenth Muse: The Psyche of the American Poet* (Cambridge, Mass., 1975), 105−11, and 45−54, 74−75, 82−83.
19. See Perry Miller's introduction to his edition of Jonathan Edwards' *Images or Shadows of Divine Things* (New Haven, 1948), 1−41, especially p. 37.
20. Gelpi, *Tenth Muse*, 110; my emphasis.

ME to be one that he hesitated to represent them or consider them as even a provisional, let alone a final, duality. But when it came to correspondence, insisting on one distinction—that between ME and NOT-ME—prevented Emerson from admitting or using another—that between ME and God, or human and divine.

Not being able to make use of this distinction between human and divine ordinarily made no difference to Emerson. On the contrary, his affirmations of compensation and self-reliance derive their strength from Emerson's brooking no merely human self as his quester or his hero, but rather practicing divinities. But when it comes to celebrating correspondence, especially in *Nature*, Emerson's disinclination to conceive of a humanity distinct from divinity does make a difference. When it comes to correspondence, Emerson's message—that the world is the language of the spirit—puts a particular strain on his form. This is because correspondence is a different order of principle from compensation and self-reliance. In affirming compensation and self-reliance, Emerson affirms cosmic principles, principles of the ME that appear as costs in the NOT-ME. The workings of compensation and self-reliance are such that nature confirms spirit in experience of loss, diminution, or cost. As a language, however, correspondence is already a confirmation, already a cost, because it is a result—the result of a separation. This difference between correspondence and the other two principles becomes evident when Emerson affirms correspondence by celebrating its ramifications, for he finds these ramifications to be not costly but enriching. The riches of correspondence are an embarrassment, because they are the promise and power that should belong exclusively to the uncreated, but are in fact part of creation. For correspondence says that nature is the language of spirit, and as a language, nature can taint or confound spirit as well as reveal it. Which one it does depends on proper interpretation. Thus, celebrating this principle of correspondence whereby nature is both made and interpretable—indeed, is designed to be interpreted—commits Emerson to celebrating reciprocity with the uncreated instead of union with the uncreated. There is something especially attractive in the promise of correspondence, at

least for a lover of literature and language. There is the suggestion that nothing sensible is without its supersensible counterpart, that everywhere one looks is readable script waiting to be
interpreted. *Nature* is Emerson's celebration of nature as the language of the uncreated, but despite the promise of correspondence, questions arise. Does Emerson celebrate nature as utterance or as text? Does he celebrate authorship or interpretation,
authority or interpretability. I want to show that Emerson's fear
of confounding these and his hope of relating them find expression in the delicacies and difficulties that characterize his lyrical
manifesto, *Nature*.

In *Nature* Emerson affirms the power of correspondence. Correspondence makes the NOT-ME a text to be interpreted by the
ME, and it makes that interpretation reveal the existence and the
power of the ME. In affirming correspondence, then, Emerson affirms the readability of a figurative universe; he affirms that nature is a scripture whose types and tropes may be read by a fit
reader. It is clear that this is the dynamic of correspondence that
concerns Emerson most in *Nature*. At least until *Nature*'s final
chapters, "original relation" means reading the universe much
more often than it means writing the universe. Textuality and
interpretability dominate Emerson's affirmations of correspondence in *Nature*. Indeed, as we observed in the discussion of "Behavior" and language in Chapter I, the readability of language,
including the availability of fit readers, remained important in
Emerson's thinking and in his articulations of it. Of course what
makes any text interpretable is that it is taken as figurative.
Emerson affirmed the figurative power of language. Even this implicit definition of utterance, from the "Language" chapter of
Nature, treats utterance as a process of connecting rather than
making: "A man's power to connect his thought with its proper
symbol, *and so to utter it*, depends on the simplicity of his character, that is upon his love of truth and his desire to communi-
cate it without loss" (W, I, 29; CW, I, 20; my emphasis). Here
speaking is transmission enforced by intense reception more
than it is creation, and this intense reception is a kind of reading.

This interpretative responsiveness is Emerson's version of

the Romantic concern about whether poetry is conscious or inspired.[21] I am stressing here the fact that the Emersonian poet is a reader, an especially sensitive interpreter and that his creation is transmission. "The poet is . . . the man without impediment, who sees and handles that which others dream of, traverses the whole scale of experience, and is representative of man, in virtue of *being the largest power to receive and to impart*" (W, III, 6; my emphasis). That final phrase not only emphasizes reception and transmission equally, it also uses an unexpected verb—being. Emerson does not say, *having* "the largest power to receive and impart" but "*being* the largest power to receive and impart." The choice of verb underscores Emerson's idea. The poet is an instrument of reception and transmission. The poet is a conductor. What does the poet conduct? When all is said and done, "life" is by far the best answer; but whatever one decides to call what the poet conducts, *being* a conductor is his capacity, his function.

Compare that venerably Romantic sense of the poet as instrument with Emerson's other and more famous definition of the poet as "the Namer or Language-maker," naming things sometimes "after their appearance, sometimes after their existence, and giving to every one its own name and not another's thereby rejoicing the intellect which delights in detachment or boundary" (W, III, 21).

The context of this definition makes it clear that even as namer the poet is still a reader. He reads better and tells better what he reads than any other user of language, but he nevertheless is a reader before he is a speaker. In short, exalted as these conceptions of the poet are (and it is not to be forgotten that Emerson calls poets "liberating gods"—"They are free, and they make free" [W, III, 32 and 30]), they nevertheless do not describe the poet as the uncreated. Curiously, in this connection, the following sentence about the poet, from "Poetry and Imagination," comes from the section of that wonderful miscellany on the subject headed "Creation": "He knows that he did not make his

21. *Ibid.*, 79.

thought,—no, his thought made him, and made the sun and the stars." As supreme interpreter, the poet speaks and hears in figures. Indeed, "God himself does not speak prose, but communicates with us by hints, omens, inference and dark resemblances in objects lying around us" (W, VIII, 39).

As we saw earlier, the "noble doubt" that things are not things only but also figures distinguishes the philosophic or poetic mind from the common. Though Emerson never ceases to celebrate correspondence as interpretability, textuality, and interpretation, he is just as characteristically aware that such celebrations involve him in the praise of substitutions and of substituting. Consequently there is a sense in which Emerson values literal language more highly than figurative.[22] Preceding the sentence just quoted, in which Emerson acknowledges that God himself speaks in tropes, Emerson wrote, "Conversation is not permitted without tropes; nothing but great weight in things can afford a quite literal speech." The audacious preference for weighty, literal speech over the troping conversation even of God himself is perhaps only implied in that passage. Surprisingly, it becomes explicit in this one:

> There are people who can never understand a trope or any second or expanded sense given to your words, or any humor; but remain literalists, after hearing the music and poetry and rhetoric and wit of seventy or eighty years. They are past the help of surgeon or clergy. But even these can understand pitchforks and the cry of Fire! and I have noticed in some of this class a marked dislike of earthquakes. (W, VI, 140)

This is not just Emerson adding Yankee seasoning to his brand of Romantic correspondence. It is part of an epistemological and metaphysical quandary about truth and language that is caused by Emerson's faith in Romantic correspondence.[23] To affirm cor-

<hr />

22. Matthiessen, *American Renaissance*, 30–44, discusses Emerson's high regard for "the word one with the thing" and sees it as hyperbole.

23. Compare Sampson Reed in Perry Miller, ed., *The Transcendentalists: An Anthology* (Cambridge, Mass., 1950), 57: "There is a language, not of words, but of things. When this language shall have been made apparent, that which is

respondence is to affirm beauty as the manifestation of truth. Certainly Emerson's faith in this possibility and his joy in experiencing it were deep and lasting:

> A happy symbol is a sort of evidence that your thought is just. I had rather have a good symbol of my thought, or a good analogy, than the suffrage of Kant or Plato. If you agree with me, or if Locke or Montesquieu agree, I may yet be wrong; but if the elm-tree thinks the same thing, if running water, if burning coal, if crystals, if alkalies, in their several fashions say what I say, it must be true. Thus a good symbol is the best argument, and is a missionary to persuade thousands. (W, VIII, 13) [24]

Nevertheless, Emerson's trust that beauty manifested truth was in conflict (sometimes debilitating, sometimes vitalizing) with another sense of truth (and, by extension, of beauty) that had at least equal power for him. I mean his conviction that "the definition of *spiritual* should be, *that which is its own evidence.*" It should not be some rarefied degree of matter, as the pious materialist holds when he avers, "Spirit is matter reduced to an extreme thinness: O *so* thin!" (W, III, 53; Emerson's emphasis). [25]

It is no wonder that this conflict affects *Nature*. The first and

---

human will have answered its end; and being as it were resolved into its original elements, will lose itself in nature. The use of language is the expression of our feelings and desires—the manifestation of the mind. But every thing which is, whether animal or vegetable, is full of the expression of that use for which it is designed, as of its own existence. If we did but understand its language, what could our words add to its meaning? It is because we are unwilling to hear, that we find it necessary to say so much; and we drown the voice of nature with the discordant jargon of ten thousand dialects. Let a man's language be confined to the expression of that which actually belongs to his own mind; and let him respect the smallest blade which grows, and permit it to speak for itself. Then may there be poetry, which may not be written perhaps, but which may be felt as a part of our being. Everything which surrounds us is full of the utterance of one word, completely expressive of its nature. This word is its name."

24. See my discussion of troping, p. 56, herein.

25. Compare *Nature*: "Idealism acquaints us with the total disparity between the evidence of our own being and the evidence of the world's being. The one is perfect [*i.e.*, complete]; *the other, incapable of assurance*" (W, I, 62; CW, I, 37; my emphasis).

last chapters that Emerson projected for his book in his journal for January 6, 1832, were "that the mind is its own place" and "that truth is its own warrant" (JMN, III, 315–16).[26] As the actual book took shape, however, it was increasingly and definitely influenced by Coleridge, Carlyle, and Emerson's discovery of Goethe. Consequently, it became a celebration of the NOT-ME as hieroglyph of the ME and, most importantly, a celebration of the ME as the imagination Emerson elsewhere called "the reader of these forms" (W, VIII, 15). Precisely this distinction between ME as reader or interpreter and ME as author is the one that *Nature*'s argument requires, with its emphasis on the spiritually responsive imagination, but that Emerson's purpose for *Nature* resists. Emerson's purpose was to announce his "First Philosophy" of "the infinitude of the private man," and to such a purpose suggestions that the private man was exiled from the infinitude that was his home constitute impediments. Yet Emerson's subject, correspondence, continually obtruded such suggestions and considerations. As we have seen, this is because correspondence depended upon the separation between ME and NOT-ME, however much it might presage the enslavement of NOT-ME by ME. For where there is no separation, language is unnecessary as well as impossible. As "Circles" was to put it, "Good as is discourse, silence is better and shames it. The length of the discourse indicates the distance of thought betwixt the speaker and the hearer. If they were at a perfect understanding in any part, no words would be necessary thereon. If at one in all parts, no words would be suffered" (W, II, 311).

Nor does the passage that comes a few paragraphs later refute this assessment, that words are mere substitutes for knowing, doing, and being. The passage, which praises the poet, makes it clear that it is not as a bringer or user of language that the poet is valued but only as one whose language is at least less discursive than that of "the encyclopaedia, or the treatise on metaphysics, or the Body of Divinity" (W, III, 312). One could multiply instances of Emerson's mistrust of language as being either too discursive or too seductively figurative; and one could multiply,

26. Sealts and Ferguson (eds.), *Emerson's* Nature, 38–39.

probably to a matching extent, instances of Emerson's faith that language enabled the eloquence that was divinity. It is not important that Emerson could feel two different and inconsistent ways about one phenomenon—especially one so complex as language. Instead, what matters is that language is both literal and figurative for Emerson. Not alternately, but at the same time. For the author it is literal, for the interpreting reader it is figurative. This metaphysical and epistemological volatility is the reciprocity that complicates Emersonian correspondence, as adequate desire and responsive motivation complicate, respectively, Emersonian compensation and self-reliance.

As WE have seen throughout this discussion of *Nature* and original relation, the *fact* of correspondence interests Emerson primarily because of the *act* of correspondence that it presages, requires, and enables. In order to celebrate the fact of correspondence, Emerson is always mindful of the distinctions that are the foundations of that fact, especially the distinction between ME and NOT-ME. The "Discipline" chapter of *Nature* summarizes Emerson's respect for distinctions this way: "Therefore is Space, and therefore Time, that man may know that things are not huddled and lumped, but sundered and individual" (W, I, 38; CW, I, 24). At the same time, using distinctions as borders to be crossed was even more important to Emerson than making or perceiving them. His affirmations of correspondence involve him in such crossings just as much as they involve him in maintaining the distinctions that occasion those crossings.

So vigorous and volatile is the reciprocity of Emersonian correspondence that it amounts to self-referentiality. Self-referentiality is the extreme form of correspondence's essential volatility. The very terms *uncreated* and NOT-ME illustrate this, as we have seen. When Emerson defines "nature," nature is a negative, and when he defines "spirit," spirit is. By this fiat, Emerson announces in each case what is to be axiomatic and what derived. Emerson thereby makes the axiomatic and the derived interchangeable, as well as distinct. That paradoxical achievement is another way of indicating the radical self-referentiality of Emersonian correspondence.

In *Nature*, especially in its fourth chapter, "Language," Emerson tries to capture the volatility that is the essence of his idea of correspondence; and he tries to clarify the self-referentiality that is the extreme form of this volatility. His second through his fifth chapters all describe the ways the NOT-ME serves the ME. Having devoted a chapter each to nature as commodity and as beauty, Emerson now declares, "Language is a third use which Nature subserves to man. Nature is the vehicle of thought in a simple, double, and three-fold degree" (W, I, 25; CW, I, 27). Just as beauty is a use to which the ME may put the NOT-ME, so language is, too. Like beauty, language also serves as type, to suggest the possibilities or the existence of the uncreated; and it serves as trope, to reflect these. In a March, 1836, journal note Emerson articulates this idea. Compare the predication that Emerson chooses for each of his three subjects as he does so. "Thus through Nature is there a striving upward. Commodity points to a greater good. Beauty is nought until the spiritual element. Language refers to that which is to be said" (JMN, V, 146 and n. 442).

Notice that when "language" is the subject the predicate becomes circular; and notice that this circularity is apt. "Language refers to that which is to be said." As I have argued, self-referentiality is the ultimate form of the volatile reciprocity that complicates correspondence. The fact that this self-referentiality is a complication is borne out when one observes that the self-referentiality of language constitutes the subject of *Nature*'s fourth chapter more than it constitutes the chapter's form. For instance the well-known list that opens the chapter makes the self-referentiality of language no clearer than does the more gnomic journal entry just quoted. Here, for reference, is the list:

1. Words are signs of natural facts.
2. Particular natural facts are symbols of particular spiritual facts.
3. Nature is the symbol of spirit.

Despite their precise format these assertions manage to seem both confusing and redundant. The elaborations that follow do dispel the confusion and the impression of redundancy, for Emerson proceeds to clarify that he has a reason for separating words as signs from facts as symbols; he wishes to stress that the second category of correspondence includes the first. Similarly, the elaboration of the third assertion does detail the self-referentiality of language, but Emerson's discussion makes it seem as if he himself is not quite sure that self-referentiality is the essential subject of his exposition at this point. When Emerson comes to elaborate the third item in his list he seems at first merely to be summarizing, but it is soon evident that the very fact that signs signify is itself emblematic: "Parts of speech are metaphors, because the whole of nature is a metaphor of the human mind" (W, I, 32; CW, I, 21). That is to say, troping is itself a type. Of what? Of the human mind, or the uncreated. It is a type of the way the uncreated works. And how does the uncreated work? By creating, by uttering, by symbolization, as we saw in Chapter III. In short, Emerson's three-paragraph elaboration of his third assertion attempts to explain how nature serves as language in being "the symbol of spirit." But the explanation never exceeds in clarity or range his paradoxical journal note on the same topic: "Language refers to that which is to be said."

If my interpretation of Emerson's elaboration is correct, we are in what Rosalie Colie has called "the hall of mirrors of paradoxical speculation." Colie is referring to paradoxy's being based in self-referentiality, and she is also suggesting the intellectual temptations that attend that fact.[27] The Emersonian blurring of type and trope that Albert Gelpi studies in *The Tenth Muse* may be regarded as part of Emerson's Neo-Platonic, transcendentalist habit of paradox. Though paradox is, as Rosalie Colie has demonstrated, "at once a figure of speech and figure of thought,"[28] and though Emerson is certainly adept at paradox as a figure of speech, in *Nature* paradox is more a figure of thought than a figure of speech. I think *Nature*'s paucity of paradoxical forms argues that Emerson was not aware of how paradoxical his message about language (or about nature) really was. *Nature*'s speciously discursive organization into chapters, with their

27. Colie, *Paradoxia Epidemica*, xv; and see her index, under "self-assurance."
28. *Ibid.*, 508.

numbered sections, which promise a symmetry or clarity that does not occur, argues the same thing. So does Emerson's apparent difficulty in deciding whether the best speech is the most picturesque (W, I, 30; CW, I, 20) or the most literal. I say "apparent difficulty" because there is no doubt that Emerson *believes* literal speech to be the most pictorial and *vice versa*; but the surface features of the text do not support or reveal this conviction. Rather, the obdurate paradoxy of Emerson's various assertions about correspondence is necessitated by *Nature*'s argument, but not revealed by *Nature*'s form.

Emerson's vehemence when he describes the third and most paradoxical degree of the ways in which nature is vehicle of thought should be fully noticed in this connection. The surprisingly antagonistic tone that he suddenly adopts at this point is a signal that the common underreading of the natural fact called language causes Emerson distress:

> But how great a language to convey such peppercorn informations! Did it need such noble races of creatures, this profusion of forms . . . to furnish man with the dictionary and grammar of his municipal speech? [Is troping the only use we know to make of the manifold correspondences all about us? Are we not able to see each single one as a type of how the uncreated works, and see all their multiplicity as type of how thoroughly the uncreated works this way?[29] We are not, as the rest of this passage plainly says:] Whilst we use this grand cipher to expedite the affairs of our pot and kettle, we feel that we have not yet put it to its use, neither are we able. We are like travellers using the cinders of a volcano to roast their eggs. . . . Have mountains, and waves, and skies no significance but what we consciously give them when we employ them as emblems of our thoughts? (W, I, 32; CW, I, 21)

Of course they have more significance. They are types of divine thoughts, not just human ones. Thus they are reminders of a separation between humanity and divinity that Emerson did not or-

29. Cf. Gelpi, *Tenth Muse*, 106.

dinarily insist upon, even when he credited it at all. Unrecognized, this "three-fold degree" in which "nature is the vehicle of thought" is a wasted opportunity. It is an access ignored. Recognized for the bridge that it is, it is evidence of the gap to be spanned.

Most of us are too parochial to acknowledge the third degree of the ways nature is emblem of spirit, let alone benefit from using it fully. Emerson again uses this image of a misunderstood gift of fire when he presents this same limitation in the first paragraph of "The Poet," this time ventriloquistically: "It is a proof of the shallowness of the doctrine of beauty as it lies in the minds of our amateurs, that men seem to have lost the perception of the instant dependence of form upon soul. . . . We were put into our bodies as fire is put into a pan to be carried about" (W, III, 3). So we are prone to think; but of course, as "the highest minds in the world know," we are mistaken. "Orpheus, Empedocles, Heraclitus, Plato, Plutarch, Dante, Swedenborg"—these minds are responsive to the manifold analogies with spiritual fact that every natural fact provides. However rare such interpreters may be, they are possible. They are possible because, "we are not pans and barrows, nor even porters of the fire and torch-bearers, but children of the fire, made of it, and only the same divinity transmuted and at two or three removes, when we know least about it" (W, III, 3). We are not tropes for the fire, we are types of the fire. In this case Emerson is not blurring the distinction between trope and type but insisting on it.

The situation is perfectly circular: Since human beings, at least the best ones, are able to read nature as a text of their own divinity, they are the "same divinity transmuted" as the divine fire that created them. What dictates that the ability to read nature makes you one with its author is "the fundamental law of criticism" that Emerson quotes from George Fox: "'Every scripture is to be interpreted by the same spirit which gave it forth'" (W, I, 35; CW, I, 23). George Fox's rule affirms that interpretation is the result of a radical sympathy between reader and author. The confirmations of this promising radical sympathy emphasize its rarity rather than its valuable result: "If we meet no gods, it is because we harbor none" (W, VI, 230); or, as Emerson's Orphic poet puts it in *Nature*, "What we are, that only can we see" (W, I, 76; CW, I, 45).[30]

Those confirmations and that affirmation agree that our interpretations both create what we know and are created by what we know. Interpretations are thus both a what and a how. Interpretation is epistemological, showing us how we know, and metaphysical, showing us what we know, or what *to* know. For Emerson such a circular situation was not vicious. It was benign; for he regarded circularity as circulation that sustained, not as a constriction that thwarted. For Emerson the circularity of self-reference was to be cultivated, not shunned. To him, the tautologies of paradoxy were not "the prison house of language" that Frederic Jameson, quoting Nietzsche, finds formalistic poetics to be.[31] Jameson astutely describes the self-referentiality of structuralism and Russian formalism. At the same time he criticizes the self-validation and self-absorption that such self-referentiality serves, in his view, to foster. Jameson is particularly concerned to demonstrate that structuralist thought is "structurally incapable of evolving a theory of self-consciousness" and that without such a "theory of its own particular situation . . . some basic explanation of its own knowledge any philosophy is doomed to make itself its object *without detecting that it is doing so.*"[32] As emblem of this dangerous kind of situation, Jameson quotes James Thurber's funny and harrowing description of his attempts to learn how to look through a microscope in botany class. In the anecdote Thurber is at last able to see something, and he draws it as he has been required to do. "But the instructor is not as satisfied as the student with the drawing that results. 'That's your eye!' he shouted. 'You've drawn your eye!'"[33]

In his Marxist critique of the self-validating, self-referentiality

30. Compare "The Poet" (W, III, 15): "Since everything in nature answers to a moral power, if any phenomenon remains brute and dark it is because the corresponding faculty in the observer is not active."

31. See Frederic Jameson, *The Prison-House of Language: A Critical Account of Structuralism and Russian Formalism* (Princeton, 1972).

32. *Ibid.*, 207–208; my emphasis.

33. *Ibid.*, 206–207.

of various formalistic poetics, Jameson holds that a self-referential structure is structurally incapable of self-consciousness and therefore of self-criticism: "It cannot perform the most basic function of self-consciousness, which is to . . . reckon the place of the observer into the experiment, to put an end to the infinite regression [which characteristically embarrasses it]."[34] In her book on paradox Rosalie Colie frequently uses this same image of infinite regression (or progression) to characterize self-referentiality, which is the basis of all paradoxy. But though Colie likens paradoxy to a seductive hall of mirrors with its vortex of "infinite alternatives," she also explains how paradoxes can work self-critically by virtue of their self-referentiality:

> Paradox deals with itself as subject and as object, and in this respect too may be seen as both tautological and paradoxical. Particular paradoxes, especially logical and mathematical paradoxes, are often "fixed" into adamantine hardness, because they mark a regular edge to progressive thinking, a point at which "object" turns into "subject." The thinking process, examining for the "error" which brought it up sharp against paradox, turns back on itself to see how it got stuck upon the paradox, and if that paradox might have been avoided: a paradox generates the self-referential activity. Operating at the limits of discourse, redirecting thoughtful attention to the faulty or limited structures of thought, paradoxes play back and forth across terminal and categorical boundaries.[35]

To be sure Jameson would consider Colie's assertions part of the problem, not part of the solution, since the final pages of his critical account argue that "a theory of models cannot recognize itself for a model without undoing the very premises on which it is itself founded."[36] I do not presume to answer Jameson's critique of self-referentiality—not even with Rosalie Colie's expert words on the subject. Rather, I want to use Jameson's account of the dangers of self-reference, and Colie's understanding of its

34. *Ibid.*, 208.
35. Colie, *Paradoxia Epidemica*, xv and 7.
36. Jameson, *The Prison-House of Language*, 208, and see 207–16.

characteristics as a context for my examination of how Emerson himself deals with the self-referential dynamics of correspondence that he insists upon.

Instead of asking whether Emerson should mistrust the self-referentiality of his version of correspondence more than he does, and instead of asking why he does not mistrust it more, I observe that he does not mistrust it. Characteristically, he neither trusts nor mistrusts, because Emerson characteristically does not seek validation. As we saw in Chapter IV, the Emersonian quest is undertaken within certainty, not in search of certainty; and it is a quest after power, not after truth. Rather than seeking to determine the truth, Emerson seeks the life to match the truth. He seeks vitality. The quest after vitality is always complete, never finished, as we have seen. Consequently, the movement it requires is not linear. Even circular or spiral movement does not quite cover the kind of movement proper to the Emersonian quest within certainty, because those are spatial movements. Instead of circular movement, circulatory movement is what Emerson values, seeks, and wants to bring about. Such movement is not so much spatial as transformational. Whether such circulatory movement is thought of as systole and diastole, a breathing, or as some other expansion and contraction, does not matter. What does matter is that an alternation or a circularity or a volatility that might in other imaginations seem futile or self-serving, or simply frivolous, can become sources of what is valuable in this quest: vitality. Moreover, they become ways to avoid what threatens in this quest: complacency, numbness, lethe.

Emerson is a vitalist, whatever else he is. Though vitalism is, according to *The Harper Dictionary of Modern Thought*, "a miscellany of beliefs," these are "united by the contention that living processes are not to be explained in terms of the material composition and physico-chemical performances of living bodies."[37] Of course the philosophical controversy among biologists between the so-called dogmatic vitalists, according to whom "living things are animated by a vital principle such as an en-

---

37. *The Harper's Dictionary of Modern Thought*, ed. Alan Bullock and Oliver Stallybrass (New York, 1977), 666.

telechy . . . or *elan vital*," and the mechanists, according to whom one's methodology must be to behave "*as if* all vital activities could be explained in terms of material composition and physico-chemical performance," was more than half a century away when Emerson published *Nature*.[38] Nevertheless a Heraclitean world in which flux enlivens and stagnation destroys appealed to Emerson's rebellious temper. Moreover, such a "standard of energy" to adopt the title of Martin Price's chapter on Blake's vitalism)[39] seemed to be an effective transvaluation of the standard of adherence preferred by dogmatists of all kinds, including materialists.

Fundamentally, Emerson's taste for vitalism contrasts less with any sort of mechanism or materialism than with his own faith in the absolute stability and independence of the uncreated. "Every correspondence we observe in mind and matter suggests a substance older and deeper than either of these old nobilities" (W, VIII, 9). That absolutely unwavering conviction directs all Emerson's dynamic and relativistic enthusiasm for flux and circulation. In "Idealism" he calls the uncreated the "thoughts of the Supreme Being" and goes on to define their uncaused causing with these lines, which he adapted from Proverbs:[40] "These are they who were set up from everlasting, from the beginning, or ever the earth was. When he prepared the heavens, they were there; when he established the clouds above, when he strengthened the fountains of the deep. Then they were by him as one brought up with him. Of them took he counsel" (W, I, 56–57; CW, I, 34).

Emerson's vitalism is teleological and so it complements the absolutism with which it conflicts in him. In Proverbs, *wisdom* is the antecedent of *these* and *them*, but Emerson omits the antecedent name. The omission accords with his rhetoric of ineffability. He prefers to retain only the Orphic chanting in his description of these world-creating ideas. His vitalism makes his

38. *Ibid.* For a discussion of the controversy, see Jan Romein, *The Watershed of Two Eras: Europe in 1900*, transl. Arnold Pomerans (Middletown, Conn., 1978), 340–53.

39. Martin Price, *To the Palace of Wisdom* (New York, 1964).

40. Proverbs VIII: 23, 27, 28, 30. And see W, I, 57, n. 1, and CW, I, 252.

faith in design less doctrinaire, and his faith in design makes his vitalism more substantial than either would be alone. Jan Romein's summary of the doctrine of holism, which so-called dogmatic vitalists brought to biology at the turn of the century, serves admirably to describe Emerson's teleological vitalism: "Holists made 'the principle of life' a cardinal principle and, moreover, one . . . of which it was impossible to say whether it worked *in* matter, *on* matter, *through* matter, or *with the help of* matter."[41] With its emphasis on locational and relational elusiveness, that description fits the volatility of Emerson's teleological vitalism. My point in calling Emerson a vitalist and developing the notion thus anachronistically has not been to hold that Emerson's use of his avid reading in science and philosophy made him the prophet of a conflict in the philosophy of science. Rather, in calling Emerson a vitalist and adducing these descriptions of what the term later came to cover, I have intended to illuminate and characterize what is valuable and what inimical in the Emersonian quest, the quest within certainty. With this extended view of Emerson as a vitalist, we may return to *Nature*.

NEITHER IN *Nature* nor elsewhere in his work does Emerson emphasize nature's organic life. Nature is an animated still-life for Emerson, a fable, a "mute gospel" (W, I, 42; CW, I, 26). It is not to be investigated but rather to be interpreted, experienced, responded to. Nature can be a stimulus to him, and a support; but Emerson has little interest in studying nature, though the studies of others contributed a cherished supply of fables to his thinking and writings. To be sure, this response is to be expected of one who sees nature as something made or composed rather than as something which just grows, but the absence of passages about nature's independent organic life, particularly vegetable life, seems striking nonetheless. Amid the memorable passages about stars, sunsets, farms, landscapes, horizons, *Nature*'s most memorable reference to vegetable life is surely the sentence that Christopher Cranch's famous drawing memorialized by caricature: "I have no hostility to Nature but a child's love of it, I expand and

41. Romein, *The Watershed of Two Eras*, 350–51; Romein's emphasis.

grow in the warm day like corn and melons" (W, I, 59; CW, I, 35).[42] Cranch's cartoon may be caricaturing the supposed innocence or blissfulness of Emerson, but Emerson seems to me to be writing caricature himself in the sentence about corn and melons. He seems to be contrasting the complacency of the blissful but mindless vegetable expansion with the demanding openness that he really values. For the vigorous mindfulness Emerson values, images from physiology or zoology serve him much better and more frequently than do images of trees, plants, flowers, or harvests.

An example is Emerson's use in *Nature* of his epiphanic experience at the Jardin des Plantes during his first European trip: "In a cabinet of natural history, we become sensitive of a certain occult recognition and sympathy in regard to . . . that wonderful congruity which subsists between man and the world" (W, I, 67–68; CW, I, 40). A less well-known but even more typical example is the following passage from "The Individual," the final lecture in the Philosophy of History series, which concerns the individual as a point of view:

> Physiology affords some striking examples of this fact, that knowledge dissipates fear . . . in the discovery that the internal organs which we are accustomed to think exquisitely alive to pain, are actually without any external sensibility. The skin is endued with its extreme sensibility as a necessary warning to the whole body of approaching harm. The internal muscles and ligaments of the limbs, when laid bare are quite callous to the touch, because a sensibility to touch in organs which are always covered would avail nothing.[43]

Emerson's organicism cannot usually be accommodated by vegetable images because his organicism includes not just harmony but purpose, and not just obedience but motivation.[44] In an 1837 journal entry Emerson sets down the fragment, "The

42. The drawing is most conveniently available in Sherman Paul, *Emerson's Angle of Vision.*

43. EL, II, 182 and n. 17.

44. The fablelike image of the banian tree at the end of "Compensation" could be considered an example of an exception. See W, I, 126–27, and Chapter IV, p. 100, herein.

kingdom of the involuntary, of the not me" (JMN, V, 333); and in 1846 he enters the following prayer for eloquence which later finds a place in "Poetry and Imagination": "O celestial Bacchus! drive them mad,—this multitude of vagabonds, hungry for eloquence, hungry for poetry, starving for symbols, perishing for want of *electricity to vitalize this too much pasture*" (JMN, VII, 215; W, VIII, 70).[45]

Vitalizing this too much pasture is Emerson's mission as it is his preoccupation. No one can read *Nature*'s sixth chapter, "Spirit," without seeing how completely Emerson equates spirit, and not nature, with life. Vitalizing means spiritualizing and spiritualizing means vitalizing. As we saw in the discussion of Emerson's fables and other rhetorical "leasts," utterance both manifests spirit and transmits spirit. As we have seen in the present chapter on the ways *Nature* dramatizes correspondence, utterance seems to be one use of language while interpretation of the text that such utterance creates seems to be another. The uncreated creates correspondence; the created—*including* human beings—both *is* that corresponding text and *reads* or *interprets* that corresponding text. I distinguish between authoring and interpreting in this chapter, because it seems to me that Emerson does so, especially in *Nature*. Interpretability and interpretation figure far more than does speaking (or writing) in Emerson's affirmations of correspondence, and this is so because correspondence is a principle that depends on the NOT-ME. It is a property of the NOT-ME, in contrast to self-reliance and compensation, which manifest in the NOT-ME but belong to the ME, or uncreated.

In fact, not until *Nature*'s final chapters, "Spirit" and "Prospects," does Emerson give primacy to speaking: Nature "always speaks of spirit," he writes in the penultimate chapter. Then, after emphasizing the ineffability of spirit, which "refuses to be recorded in propositions," he proceeds to tell in what sense nature can be said to speak and with what purpose. Nature "is the great organ through which the universal spirit speaks to the indi-

45. Recall, too, the passage from "Wealth" about the scholar going to his garden for refreshment and finding confusion instead.

vidual, *and strives to lead back the individual to it"* (W, I, 62; CW, I, 37; my emphasis). The clause I have italicized reconciles the idea of nature as text with the idea of interpretation as divinization.

Emerson opens the chapter on spirit with a clear statement that divinization is its central idea: "It is essential to a true theory of nature and of man that it should contain somewhat progressive" (W, I, 61; CW, I, 36). But he does not feel free to develop this idea right away. Instead, he recapitulates the argument of "Idealism" in order to emphasize two points. First, idealism can answer only the question, "What is matter?" not the more important questions of "Whence is it and Whereto?" (W, I, 62; CW, I, 37). Second, though the limits of idealism are the famous one that "it leaves God out of me" and "leaves me in the splendid labyrinth of my perceptions, to wander without end" (W, I, 63; CW, I, 37), it does at least serve "to apprize us of the eternal distinction between the soul and the world" (W, I, 63; CW, I, 38). Only when Emerson has re-emphasized these two points does he feel free to develop the idea of melioration to which he wants to devote his chapter on spirit.

The whence and whereto that constitute the progressiveness of spirit are circular, or rather circulatory. "Spirit creates" is what we learn when we learn to think on those questions of whence and whereto, which are questions of original relation. What does spirit create? Nature. And how does spirit create? "Spirit . . . does not build up nature around us, but puts it forth through us, as the life of the tree puts forth new branches and leaves through the pores of the old" (W, I, 64; CW, I, 38). Emerson's use of leaves and a tree might make some call this simile a vegetable one, and I would not wish to quibble, especially not since the next sentence begins, "As a plant upon the earth so a man rests upon the bosom of God." The difficulty is only apparent, however. Emerson goes right on to mix his metaphor: "he [man] is nourished by unfailing fountains, and draws at his need inexhaustible power," with the result, surely, that the whole becomes more an image of nurturing than of vegetable life. The "life of the tree," not its branches and leaves, is Emerson's grammatical and argumentational subject here, and the renewing force of that life as it puts forth the new through the pores of the old.

Firkins pointed out long ago that Emerson sought to be a conduit, and Joel Porte's literary portrait of Emerson, *Representative Man*, uses extensively the concept of being a conductor, especially in a specifically sexual sense as well as in a more generally physiological one.[46] Whether one thinks of being a conduit as an electrical, a spiritual, or a physiological metaphor, it unquestionably constitutes a way to avoid choosing between reception and transmission. The concept of conducting allows one to see oneself as a vehicle for circulation rather than for storage and as an agent of revitalization rather than a source liable to depletion.

In each chapter of this study I have tried to emphasize some form of Emerson's circulatory ideal. With this final chapter I have returned, in a sense, to the first one, for I have once again been concerned with language, behavior, necessity, illusion, and the regenerative conduct of life. Whether Emerson calls it the truth that is its own evidence, or nature that perpetually stands ready to figure us forth to ourselves, or life that quickens us, he is constantly speaking of a regeneration whereby the "fatal *is*" can replace the usurping "human should-or-would" (W, VIII, 30–31; hyphens mine). When it is like language that is being read, this regeneration is an experience or phenomenon. When it is like language being uttered it is a process or a substance. When it is like language itself—like the sheer possibility of interpretable creation—it is neither an experience nor a process; it is a force— a potency, a potential, a power. This renewing force is what Emerson wants to use his lyrical manifesto, *Nature*, to describe and summon and instill.

As the work of a mature man, albeit a youthful first book, *Nature* is far from merely an ebullient rhapsody, and as a lyrical manifesto *Nature* is as deeply personal as it is programmatic.

---

46. Firkins, *Ralph Waldo Emerson*, 358; Porte, *Representative Man*, 229–46 and 247–82. See also Paul, *Emerson's Angle of Vision*, 86.

Nothing is more prophetic of Emerson's lifelong imaginative program than the delicate way interpretation yields to speaking in "Spirits" and "Prospects," only to become interpretation again as Emerson renounces speaking in favor of listening—listening to his alter-author, the Orphic poet. In progressing from its emphasis upon interpretation to its emphasis upon utterance, Emerson's manifesto comes to speak about authorship. "A wise writer," he says in "Prospects" as he prepares to introduce his Orphic poet, "will feel that the ends of study and composition are best answered by announcing undiscovered regions of thought, and so communicating, through hope, new activity to the torpid spirit" (W, I, 70; CW, I, 41). Nothing could describe more plainly Emerson's message, his form, and his intention than those words. Characteristically they introduce an alter-author. Just as characteristically Emerson's alter-author makes *Nature*'s final initiative concern not the fact of correspondence but the *use* of correspondence. "A correspondent revolution in things will attend the influx of spirit" (W, I, 76; CW, I, 45).

About revolution Emerson has this to say in "History," which, incidentally, uses the metaphors of interpretation and authoring in ways parallel to *Nature*'s: "Every reform was once a private opinion, and when it shall be a private opinion again it will solve the problem of the age" (W, II, 4–5). With those eminently Emersonian words in mind, one could refashion the sentence about the correspondent revolution in things to "Every thing was once a thought and when it shall be a thought again, the revolution in things will have been accomplished." Emerson did not wish to enable the influx of spirit for its own sake but because he wished to bring about that correspondent revolution in things—transparency—which "Prospects" describes archetypally as the alignment of the axis of vision with the axis of things.

Though things were not sufficient, neither were they dispensable. This is the crux of Emersonian correspondence. As illusion, things might hide being under cover of appearance, but as creations, things awaited and invited the spirit that gave them forth and were thus confirmation of that spirit's creative power. Seen as correspondences, things then ceased to be in the saddle and ride mankind (W, IX, 78); they became instead conductors of life.

In my analysis of *Nature*'s distinctions and combinations I have insisted that correspondence and thus language is its theme. I have argued that Emerson affirms correspondence as a divisive if also creative act, that the confirming cost of correspondence is the *need* for language, and that the volatile relationship between correspondence as reading or readability and correspondence as authorship or authority constitutes the vitality if also the difficulty of this principle. This reading has perforce neglected a major thesis and image of *Nature*—vision and the seeing eye.[47] Particularly "Prospects" may seem ill served by a reading that emphasizes language, when the Orphic poet's final initiative speech says nothing of language but consists instead of the challenge to build one's own world and the commanding promise that one will be "gradually restored to perfect sight" by the "influx of spirit" that will bring about "the kingdom of man over nature" (W, I, 76 and 77; CW, I, 45).

Seeing and saying are not, however, far apart in Emerson's imagination. The same journal, "RO Mind," that shows how prayerfully wary Emerson was of confounding "what I adore with anything unworthy,"[48] contains a sentence that explicitly equates seeing and speaking when these are the regenerate and regenerating acts of reason. They are words of flat faith in the possibility of conducting life through a speech that is visionary and a vision that can be communicated. They may stand as a summary of Emerson's commanding prose. "The authority of Reason cannot be separated from its vision. They are not two acts but one. The sight commands, the command sees" (JMN, V, 272).

47. Many discussions of the importance of vision in Emerson exist. Examples include: Burke, "I, Eye, Ay—Emerson's Early Essay 'Nature'"; Richard Poirier, *A World Elsewhere: The Place of Style in American Literature* (New York, 1966), Chapter II; Joel Porte, "The Problem of Emerson," in Monroe Engel (ed.), *Uses of Literature* (Cambridge, Mass., 1973), 101–105; Tanner, *The Reign of Wonder*, Chapter 2; and, of course, Paul, *Emerson's Angle of Vision, passim.*
48. See, p. 146, herein.

Bibliography

BOOKS

Barfield, Owen. *Saving the Appearances: A Study in Idolatry*. London: Faber and Faber, 1959.

Berry, Edmund G. *Emerson's Plutarch*. Cambridge, Mass.: Harvard University Press, 1961.

Bishop, Jonathan. *Emerson on the Soul*. Cambridge, Mass.: Harvard University Press, 1964.

Bloom, Harold. *Figures of Capable Imagination*. New York: Seabury Press, 1976.

————. *The Ringers in the Tower*. Chicago: University of Chicago Press, 1971.

Booth, Wayne. *The Rhetoric of Fiction*. Chicago: University of Chicago Press, 1961.

Buell, Lawrence I. *Literary Transcendentalism: Style and Vision in the American Renaissance*. Ithaca, N.Y.: Cornell University Press, 1973.

Burroughs, John. *Birds and Poets*. Boston and New York: Houghton Mifflin and Co., 1891.

Cameron, Kenneth Walter. *Emerson Among His Contemporaries: A Harvest of Estimates, Insights, and Anecdotes from the Victorian Literary World, and an Index*. Hartford, Conn.: Transcendental Books, 1967.

————. *Emerson's Workshop*. 2 vols.; Hartford, Conn.: Transcendental Books, 1964.

————. *Ralph Waldo Emerson's Reading*. Raleigh, N.C.: Thistle Press, 1941.

Carlyle, Thomas. *Sartor Resartus*. Edited by Charles Frederick Harrold. New York: Odyssey Press, 1937.

Carpenter, Frederick Ives. *Emerson and Asia*. Cambridge, Mass.: Harvard University Press, 1930.

Chapman, John Jay. *Emerson and Other Essays*. New York: Charles Scribner's Sons, 1898.

Charvat, William. *Emerson's American Lecture Engagements: A Chronological List*. New York: New York Public Library, 1961.

Chatman, Seymour, ed. *Approaches to Poetics.* New York and London: Columbia University Press, 1973.

Colie, Rosalie L. *Paradoxia Epidemica: The Renaissance Tradition of Paradox.* Princeton, N.J.: Princeton University Press, 1966.

Cowan, Michael H. *City of the West: Emerson, America, and Urban Metaphor.* New Haven and London: Yale University Press, 1967.

Dewey, John. "Emerson." In *Characters and Events.* New York: Henry Holt and Co., 1929.

Dickinson, Emily. *Poems of Emily Dickinson.* Edited by Thomas H. Johnson. Cambridge, Mass.: Belknap Press of Harvard University Press, 1951.

Emerson, Ralph Waldo. *The Collected Works of Ralph Waldo Emerson.* Vol. 1: *Nature, Addresses, and Lectures.* Edited by Robert E. Spiller and Alfred R. Ferguson. Cambridge, Mass.: Harvard University Press, 1971.

———. *The Complete Works of Ralph Waldo Emerson.* 12 vols.; Edited by Edward W. Emerson. Centenary Edition, Boston and New York: Houghton, Mifflin and Co., 1903–1904.

———. *The Early Lectures of Ralph Waldo Emerson.* Edited by Stephen E. Whicher, et al. 3 vols.; Cambridge, Mass.; Belknap Press of Harvard University Press, 1959, 1964, 1972.

———. *The Journals and Miscellaneous Notebooks of Ralph Waldo Emerson.* Edited by William H. Gilman, *et al.* 14 vols. to date. Cambridge, Mass.: Harvard University Press, 1960—.

———. *The Journals of Ralph Waldo Emerson.* Edited by Edward W. Emerson and Waldo Emerson Forbes. 10 vols.; Boston and New York: Houghton Mifflin and Co., 1909–1914.

Feidelson, Charles Jr. *Symbolism and American Literature.* Chicago: University of Chicago Press, 1953.

Firkins, Oscar W. *Ralph Waldo Emerson.* Boston: Houghton Mifflin, Riverside Press, 1915.

Fish, Stanley. *Surprised by Sin: The Reader in* Paradise Lost. New York and London: St. Martin's Press and Macmillan, 1967.

———. *Self-Consuming Artifacts.* Berkeley and Los Angeles: University of California Press, 1972.

Frye, Northrop. *Anatomy of Criticism.* 1957; rpt. Princeton, N.J.: Princeton University Press, 1971.

Gelpi, Albert. *The Tenth Muse: The Psyche of the American Poet.* Cambridge, Mass., and London: Harvard University Press, 1975.

Gonnaud, Maurice. *Individu et Société dans L'Oeuvre de Ralph Waldo Emerson: Essai de Biographie Spirituelle.* Paris: Didier, 1964.

Harding, Walter. *Emerson's Library*. Published for the Biographical Society of the University of Virginia. Charlottesville, Va.: University of Virginia Press, 1967.

Hartman, Geoffrey H. *Wordsworth's Poetry: 1787–1814*. New Haven and London: Yale University Press, 1964.

Hawkes, Terence. *Structuralism and Semiotics*. Berkeley and Los Angeles: University of California Press, 1977.

Hoffman, Daniel. *Form and Fable in American Fiction*. New York: Oxford University Press, 1965.

Hopkins, Vivian C. *The Spires of Form: A Study of Emerson's Aesthetic Theory*. Cambridge, Mass.: Harvard University Press, 1951.

James, Henry. "Emerson." In *Partial Portraits*. London and New York: Macmillan and Co., 1888. Rpt. in Henry James, *The Art of Fiction and Other Essays*. New York: Oxford University Press, 1948.

Jameson, Frederic. *The Prison-House of Language: A Critical Account of Structuralism and Russian Formalism*. Princeton, N.J.: Princeton University Press, 1972.

Konvitz, Milton R. and Stephen E. Whicher, eds. *Emerson: A Collection of Critical Essays*. Englewood Cliffs, N.J.: Prentice Hall, 1962.

Kouwenhoven, John. *The Beer Can by the Highway*. Garden City, N.Y.: Doubleday, 1961.

Levin, David, ed. *Emerson: Prophecy, Metamorphosis, and Influence*. New York, Columbia University Press, 1975.

Macdonald, George. *A Hidden Life and Other Poems*. New York: Scribner's, 1872.

Matthiessen, F. O. *American Renaissance: Art and Expression in the Age of Emerson and Whitman*. New York: Oxford University Press, 1941.

Melville, Herman. *The Confidence Man: His Masquerade*. New York: Holt, Rinehart and Winston, Inc., 1964.

Miles, Josephine. *Ralph Waldo Emerson*. University of Minnesota Pamphlets on American Writers, No. 41, 1964.

Miller, Perry. Introduction to *Images or Shadows of Divine Things*, by Jonathan Edwards. New Haven: Yale University Press, 1948.

———. *Nature's Nation*. Cambridge, Mass.: Belknap Press of Harvard University Press, 1967.

———, ed. *The Transcendentalists: An Anthology*. Cambridge, Mass.: Harvard University Press, 1950.

Packer, B. L. *Emerson's Fall: A New Interpretation of the Major Essays*. New York: Continuum, 1982.

Paul, Sherman. *Emerson's Angle of Vision: Man and Nature in American Experience.* Cambridge, Mass.: Harvard University Press, 1952.
————. *The Shores of America.* Urbana: University of Illinois Press, 1958.

Poirier, Richard. *A World Elsewhere: The Place of Style in American Literature.* New York: Oxford University Press, 1966.

Porte, Joel. *Emerson and Thoreau: Transcendentalists in Conflict.* Middletown, Conn.: Wesleyan University Press, 1966.
————. *Representative Man: Ralph Waldo Emerson in His Time.* New York: Oxford University Press, 1979.

Price, Martin. *To the Palace of Wisdom.* New York: Doubleday & Co., Inc., 1964.

Romein, Jan. *The Watershed of Two Eras: Europe in 1900.* Translated by Arnold J. Pomerans. Middletown, Conn.: Wesleyan University Press, 1978.

Rourke, Constance. *American Humor: A Study of the National Character.* 1931; rpt. Garden City, N.Y.: Doubleday and Co., Anchor Books, 1955.

Rusk, Ralph L., ed. *The Letters of Ralph Waldo Emerson.* 6 vols.; New York and London: Columbia University Press, 1939.

Sealts, Merton M., Jr. and Alfred R. Ferguson, eds. *Emerson's Nature—Origin, Growth, Meaning.* New York and Toronto: Dodd, Mead & Company, Inc., 1969.

Sewall, Richard B. *The Life of Emily Dickinson.* 2 vols.; New York: Farrar, Straus, and Giroux, 1974.

Simons, Myron and Thornton H. Parsons, eds. *Transcendentalism and Its Legacy.* Ann Arbor, Mich.: University of Michigan Press, 1966.

Slater, Joseph, ed. *The Correspondence of Emerson and Carlyle.* New York and London: Columbia University Press, 1964.

Stapleton, K. Laurence. *The Elected Circle: Studies in the Art of Prose.* Princeton, N.J.: Princeton University Press, 1973.

Steiner, Rudolf. *Knowledge of the Higher Worlds and Its Attainment.* London: Rudolf Steiner Press, 1963.
————. *Occult Science: An Outline.* London: Rudolf Steiner Press, 1963.

Stephen, Leslie. "Emerson." *Studies of a Biographer* (Second Series), Vol. IV; New York: G.P. Putnam, 1899–1902. Rpt. New York: Burt Franklin, 1973, pp. 130–67.

Tanner, Tony. *The Reign of Wonder: Naivety and Reality in American Literature.* London and New York: Cambridge University Press, 1965.

Thoreau, Henry David. *A Week on the Concord and Merrimack Rivers.*
Works, I. Boston and New York: Houghton Mifflin, 1906.
Waggoner, Hyatt H. *American Poets from the Puritans to the Present.*
1968; Rev. ed. Baton Rouge and London: Louisiana State Univer-
sity Press, 1983.
Whicher, Stephen E. *Freedom and Fate: An Inner Life of Ralph Waldo
Emerson.* 1953; Rpt. New York: A. S. Barnes and Co., Inc., Per-
petua edition, 1961.
————, ed. *Selections from Ralph Waldo Emerson: An Organic Anthol-
ogy.* Boston: Riverside Press, 1957.
Williams, Raymond. *Culture and Society, 1780–1950.* New York and
London: Columbia University Press, 1958. Rpt. New York: Harper
Torchbooks, 1966.
————. *Keywords: A Vocabulary of Culture and Society.* New York:
Oxford University Press, 1976.
Wills, Gary. *Nixon Agonistes: The Crisis of the Self-Made Man.* New
York: New American Library, 1971.
Yoder, R. A. *Emerson and the Orphic Poet in America.* Berkeley, Los
Angeles, London: University of California Press, 1978.

ARTICLES

Aaron, Daniel. "Emerson and the Progressive Tradition." In *Emerson:
A Collection of Critical Essays,* edited by Milton R. Konvitz and
Stephen E. Whicher. Englewood Cliffs, N.J.: Prentice Hall, 1962.
Arvin, Newton. "The House of Pain." In *Emerson: A Collection of Criti-
cal Essays,* edited by Milton R. Konvitz and Stephen E. Whicher.
Englewood Cliffs, N.J.: Prentice Hall, 1962.
Bloom, Harold. "Emerson: The Glory and Sorrows of American Roman-
ticism." *Virginia Quarterly Review,* 47 (Autumn, 1971), 546–63.
————. "The Freshness of Transformation, or Emerson on Influence."
In *Emerson: Prophecy, Metamorphosis, and Influence,* edited by
David Levin. New York: Columbia University Press, 1975.
Buell, Lawrence I. "Reading Emerson for the Structures: The Coher-
ence of the Essays." *Quarterly Review of Speech,* 58 (February,
1972), 56–69.
————. "Transcendentalist Catalogue Rhetoric: Vision Versus Form."
American Literature, 40 (1968), 325–39.
Burke, Kenneth. "I, Eye, Ay—Emerson's Early Essay 'Nature': Thoughts
on the Machinery of Transcendentalism." In *Transcendentalism*

and Its Legacy, edited by Myron Simons and Thornton H. Parsons. Ann Arbor: University of Michigan Press, 1966.

Cowley, Malcolm. "Conrad Aiken: From Savannah to Emerson." *Southern Review*, 11 (1975), 245–59.

Fish, Stanley. "Literature in the Reader: Affective Stylistics." *New Literary History*, 2 (Autumn, 1970), 123–62.

————. "What Is Stylistics and Why Are They Saying Such Terrible Things About It?" In *Approaches to Poetics*, edited by Seymour Chatman. New York and London: Columbia University Press, 1973.

Gibson, Walker. "Authors, Speakers, Readers, and Mock Readers." *College English*, 11 (February, 1950), 265–69.

Gonnaud, Maurice. "Emerson and the Imperial Self: A European Critique." In *Emerson: Prophecy, Metamorphosis, and Influence*, edited by David Levin. New York: Columbia University Press, 1975.

LaRosa, Ralph C. "Emerson's Search for Literary Form: The Early Journals." *Modern Philology*, 69, 1 (August, 1971), 25–35.

Lauter, Paul. "'Truth and Nature': Emerson's Use of Two Complex Words." *English Literary History*, 27, 1 (1960), 66–85.

Lee, Roland F. "Emerson Through Kierkegaard: Toward a Definition of Emerson's Theory of Communication." *English Literary History*, 24 (1957), 229–48.

Lloyd, Henry Demarest. "Emerson's Wit and Humor." *Forum*, 22 (November, 1896), 346–57.

M[edawar], P. B. "Vitalism." In *Harper Dictionary of Modern Thought*, edited by Alan Bullock and Oliver Stallybrass. New York: Harper and Row, 1977.

Ong, Walter J., S.J. "The Writer's Audience Is Always a Fiction." *PMLA*, 90 (January, 1975), 9–21.

Porte, Joel. "The Problem of Emerson." In *Uses of Literature*, edited by Monroe Engel. *Harvard English Studies*, 4 (1973), 85–114.

Strauch, Carl F. "Emerson's Sacred Science." *PMLA*, 73 (June, 1958), 237–50.

————. "The Importance of Emerson's Skeptical Mood." *Harvard Library Bulletin*, 11 (Winter, 1957), 117–39.

————. "The Year of Emerson's Poetic Maturity: 1834." *Philological Quarterly*, 34, 4 (October, 1955), 353–77.

Wellek, René. "Emerson and German Philosophy." *New England Quarterly*, 16, 1 (1943), 41–62.

Wyatt, David M. "Spelling Time: The Reader in Emerson's 'Circles.'" *American Literature* 48, 2 (1976), 140–51.

Yoder, R. A. "Emerson's Dialectic." *Criticism*, 11 (Fall, 1969), 313–28.

———. "Emerson—Golden Impossibility, Representative Man." *ESQ*, 21, 4 (1975), 241–59.

———. "Toward the 'Titmouse Dimension': The Development of Emerson's Poetic Style." *PMLA*, 87 (March, 1972), 255–70.

DISSERTATION

Celières, André. "The Prose Style of Emerson." Thèse Complémentaire pour le Doctorat D'Etat Presenté à la Faculté des Lettres de L'Université De Paris, 1936.

Index

Abolition of slavery, 112
Adequate desire, 37; and poverty, 39,
  57, 59, 104–105; rarity of, 46, 48
Affirmation, xi, 15, 99, 107; and con-
  firmation, xiii–xiv, 95; negative, 145
"American Scholar" address, 6, 51
"Art," 76
Arvin, Newton, 42

Barfield, Owen, 75
Beautiful Necessity, 18, 42, 61, 115
Becoming, 128–29
Behavior, 2–5, 20, 73. *See also*
  Language
"Behavior," 2–5; mentioned, 7, 13
Bishop, Jonathan, xii*n*1, 44*n*6
Bloom, Harold, 3*n*3, 22, 51, 105
Booth, Wayne, 22*n*19
Buell, Lawrence I., xv, 70, 79
Burke, Kenneth, 81*n*14
Burroughs, John, 66, 70–71

Cabot, James Eliot, 2
Carlyle, Thomas, 12, 55, 143, 154
Chapman, John Jay, 18, 21, 27
"Character," 77, 110
Chauncy, Charles. *See* Fables and
  anecdotes
"Circles," 93, 109, 128, 154
Circularity and circulation, 160, 162,
  167–68
Coleridge, Samuel Taylor, 23
Colie, Rosalie, 145, 157, 161
Compensation, 5, 6, 11, 127; and
  confirmation, 42; as principle, 96,
  131; dear to Emerson, 96–97, 131;
  and correspondence, 149
"Compensation," 96–100; and "Spir-
  itual Laws," 98; quoted, 95; men-
  tioned, xii

Conduct. *See* Behavior
Conduct of Life, The, 2–34; creates
  audience, 8, 18–27; structure of,
  19*n*14; mentioned, xii, xiv, 5,
  17, 65
Confirmation: and cost, xii–xiii, 17,
  24, 42, 62–63; and affirmation,
  xiii–xiv, 15, 95; as experience, xiii;
  and "Fate," 17; and Beautiful Necessity, 18; as proliferation, 94; and
  George Fox's rule, 159–60; and
  correspondence, 169–70
"Considerations by the Way," 32, 78
Correspondence, 5, 11, 56, 131,
  147–48, 152–53, 169–70; and fables, 69–70; as a language, 96,
  149–50, 166; of message and
  form, 127–28; self-referentiality
  of, 155
Cranch, Christopher, 164–65
"Culture," 14

"Demonology" (essay, 1877), 53, 95,
  101–103
"Demonology" (lecture, 1839), 102
Dickinson, Emily, 35–37, 45; quoted,
  35, 36, 39–40, 48, 69; mentioned,
  104, 105, 113
Disney, Walt, 86
Divinity. *See* Over-Soul
"Divinity School" address, 51, 95
Divinization, 105, 167

Elective affinities, 110–11, 121–22
Eloquence, 2–4, 87; Webster lacking,
  118. *See also* Behavior
"Eloquence" (1847), 3–4, 45, 87
"Eloquence" (1867), 72–73
Emerson, Ralph Waldo: reputation,
  xi–xii, xiv, 70; as quester, xiii, 99–

Emerson, Ralph Waldo (*continued*)
100, 105–107, 128–29, 162; and
hope, xi, xiii, xiv–xv; consolidating
power of, xiv*n*2, 70–73; aloofness
of, 7, 23, 80; skepticism of, 14, 38;
and loss, 32, 44–45, 62, 98; and
Milton, 35–37; and Montaigne,
37, 42; Orphism of, 51; and superstition, 53, 99–103, 105–107; on
Thoreau, 71–72; transcendentalism of, 81; humor of, 83–92; organicism of, 164–66; idealism of,
136–37; and German idealism,
143
—style of his essays: designed to empower, not persuade, xv, 21–24,
26–27, 73–74; beginnings and
endings, 5–7, 12, 28–29, 127–28;
abruptness, 11–12, 91; use of fables and characters, 68–70, 76, 77;
use of hyperbole, 88–91. *See also*
Fables and anecdotes; Interior oratory; Paradox; Ventriloquism
Emerson, Waldo, 44–45
"Experience," 23–25 *passim*, 35–65;
organization of, 37–38; opening
of, 38–41; mistitled, 44; contrasted with Wordsworth, 52–56;
on motivation, 115; quoted, 50;
mentioned, xii, 95, 106, 112, 126.
See also Lords of Life

Fables and anecdotes: John Quincy
Adams, 4; Aemelius, 92–93; Benedict, 75–76; Charles Chauncy, 72;
Credulous Cockayne, 86; King David, 104; gardening, 84–86; Gertrude and Blanche, 4; guttapercha,
87; Iole, 77; ironmaster, 78; Masollam the Jew, 101; Mil-Mill, 62;
Minerva, 91; sad-eyed boy, 31–32;
servants, 78–79; snow in "Illusions," 32–33; steel-filings, 49;
swimmer among drowning men,
59; Thoreau, 72; high-born Turk,
87*n*20; wicked dollar, 112–13.
See also Emerson, Ralph Waldo—
style of his essays
"Fate," 17–27; Emerson to Carlyle
on, 19; opening of, 18–20; on per-

ception, 20–21, 25–28; ending of,
22–25; compared with "Illusions,"
27–28; quoted, xii, 54, 59; men-
tioned, 109
Fate, definitions of: 24, 25–28
passim
Feidelson, Charles, 2
Firkins, Oscar W., 22*n*18, 137, 168
Fish, Stanley, 22*n*19
Fox, George, 159
"Friendship," 104
"Fugitive Slave Law Address," 116–
25; quoted, 109

Genius, 82, 132
"Give All to Love," 62, 98
God, 56, 109, 145, 167; language of,
152
Goethe, Johann Wolfgang von, 56,
101, 154
Gonnaud, Maurice, xiv*n*2

"Heroism," 103–104
"History," 129; quoted, 113, 115*n*15,
169
Hopkins, Vivian C., 83–84
Humor. *See* Emerson, Ralph Waldo
Hyperbole. *See* Emerson, Ralph
Waldo—style of his essays

Idealism, 167. *See also* Emerson,
Ralph Waldo
"Idealism." *See Nature*
Identity, 74–75, 93
"Illusions," 27–34; and "Fate," 27–
28; and *The Conduct of Life*, 28,
33; opening of, 30–31; ending of,
32–34; quoted, 41; mentioned, 65.
See also Fables and anecdotes
Immortality, 53–55, 70*n*5, 138–39
"Immortality," 51–52
"Individual, The," 165
Individualism, 107–108
Influence, 51, 54
Interior oratory, 43, 73
Interpretability, 166

James, Henry, 23
Jameson, Frederic, 160–62
Jardin des Plantes, 165

Language, 150–59; and correspondence, 96, 149; and behavior, 101, 168; and interpretability, 101, 166–69; and the textuality of *Nature*, 150–55; literal and figurative, 152, 154–55; and saying, 170. *See also* Behavior
Leasts, 66–68, 80, 89–90, 92
Lethe, 40, 56, 62, 64; in Wordsworth, as contrasted to Emerson, 52–56
"Literary Ethics," 109
Lloyd, Henry Demarest, 83–84
Lords of Life (in "Experience"): Illusion, 41–46; Temperament, 46–48; Succession, 48–51; Surfaces, 49; Surprise, 58; Subjectiveness, 57–60; Reality, 60–62; as threads, 44
"Love," 104
Lustres, 66, 118

Macdonald, George, 14
Mammoth Cave, 30–31
"Manners," 90–91
Matthiessen, F. O., 108
ME and NOT-ME, xiii, 5, 19–20; in defining nature, 138, 141–43; and post-Kantian tradition, 143–45; and negative affirmation, 145–47; related to types and tropes, 148–49; related to correspondence, 154, 166
Medal of Jove, 1, 2, 4, 20, 136
Melville, Herman, 33–34
"Memory," 56
Meter-making argument, 7
Mill, John Stuart, 23
Miller, Perry, 148
Milton, John, 35–37
Miracles. *See* Emerson, Ralph Waldo: and superstition
Montaigne, 37, 42, 50, 65
"Montaigne," 15–16; quoted, 1
Motivation, 115–16

"Natural History of Intellect," 60–61
Nature: purpose of, 60–61, 136; definition of, 137–38, 139–43; and the Uncreated, 139; as language,

150–55 *passim*; contrasted with Spirit, 166
Nature, 132–70; mistitled, 44; as manifesto, 132; audacity of, 133–34; idealism in, 136–37; questioning in, 135–36; and language, 150–55; "Language" section of, 156–57; Orphic poet in, 169; quoted, xii, xv, 133; mentioned, xii, xiv
Nietzsche, Friedrich W., 17
Noble doubt, 137, 138, 152
"Nominalist and Realist," 49, 51, 55

Ong, Walter J., 22*n*19
Openness, 126–27, 129, 130
Oratory. *See* Interior oratory
Organicism, 164–66
Original Relation, 130, 147, 150
Orthodoxy, 96–99, 113–16, 143*n*13
Orphic poet, 63–64, 169
Osman, 28, 73
Over-Soul, 92, 125, 148
"Over-Soul, The," 106, 108–10, 129

Packer, B. L., 20, 45
Paradox, 1, 4, 105; in "Wealth," 9–10; of relation between spirit and nature, 61, 136; of loss and gain, 62; of condensation and expansion, 66–68; of self-reference, 155–62; of correspondence, 157–60
Paul, Saint, xiii
Paul, Sherman, 147–48
"Philosophy of History" Series, first lecture, 109
Plato, 1, 83
"Plato," 1, 7, 83
Poet: as reporter of conversation, 74–75; as noble doubter, 138; as reader, 151; and language, 151–52, 154
"Poet, The," 106; quoted, 35, 70*n*5, 105, 159, 160*n*30
Poetic inspiration, 35–37, 39–40, 105–106, 151
"Poetry and Imagination": quoted, 50*n*11, 60, 69, 151
Polarity. *See* Paradox
Porte, Joel, xii*n*1, 168

Poverty, 57, 59, 69, 104–107
"Power," 13–14; quoted, 55, 93–94
Proverbs, 163
"Prudence," 103

Quest. *See* Emerson, Ralph Waldo

Reed, Sampson, 152*n*23
Representative Men: quoted, 49, 67, 81–82, 83
"Resources," 79–80
Rhetorical criticism, 22*n*19
Romantic movement, 59, 105, 106; and definition of *nature*, 141, 142, 143; on poetic inspiration, 151; and correspondence, 152
Rourke, Constance, 89–90

Self, 108–10
Self-reference, 155–57, 160–62
Self-reliance, xii, 5, 96, 126–27, 131; needed to read "Experience," 38; and literary influence, 50–56; as risk, 62; and compensation, 97; as God-reliance, 107, 109–10, 113–14, 125; and elective affinities, 110–11, 121–22; and sanity, 111, 124; as sovereignty, 111, 120–21; burden of, 116, 121–22; as social principle, 125–26; and individualism, 107–108; as "valid subjectivity," 108, 110
"Self-Reliance," 109, 111–16, 120–25, 125–31; and "Fugitive Slave Law" address, 116–17, 120–25; quoted, 98, 129–30
Shakespeare, William, 24, 50, 81–82; *Lear*, 60; mentioned, 133
Society, 58–59, 90–91, 111, 124
Solipsism, 59–60
Speaking, 74–76
"Sphinx, The," 135
Spirit: builds confiningly, xiii; definition of, 68, 153; and *Nature*, 166; enlivens, 166–68

"Spiritual Laws," 98, 111
Steiner, Rudolf, 26, 75*n*12
Stevens, Wallace, 59, 74, 80, 82, 147; mentioned, 86, 87, 107
Strauch, Carl F., xii*n*1
Stupendous antagonism: as definition of man, 24–25
Swedenborg, Emanuel, 67, 134, 148, 159

Thinking, 1; and production, 10; as doing, 20, 76; and physical work, 25–26
Thoreau, Henry David, 55, 71–72
"Tragic, The," 27
Transcendentalism, 81, 108*n*11
Tropes, 56; and types, 148–49, 159
Typology. *See* Tropes

Uncreated, the, 138–39, 143, 145, 146; and correspondence, 149–50, 163
Use, 20, 27, 45

Value: defined, 9
Ventriloquism, 43–45, 47–48; at ends of "Experience" and *Nature*, 63; and negative capability, 65; in "Self-Reliance," 112–14
Vitalism, 162–64, 166

"Wealth," 8–12; resemblance to "Montaigne," 15–16; on physical vs. mental work, 25; quoted, 8, 20, 84–85; mentioned, 13, 53
Webster, Daniel, 55, 117–20 *passim*
Whicher, Stephen E., xii*n*1, 60
Whitman, Walt, 105, 130
Williams, Raymond, 139–43 *passim*
Wordsworth, William, 52–56, 65
"Worship," 12–17; quoted, 52, 78, 98; mentioned, 53, 75

Yoder, R. A., xii*n*1, 51, 66*n*1

	DATE DUE		
OCT 2 8 1999			
MAY 0 9 1994			
NOV 0 1 1994			